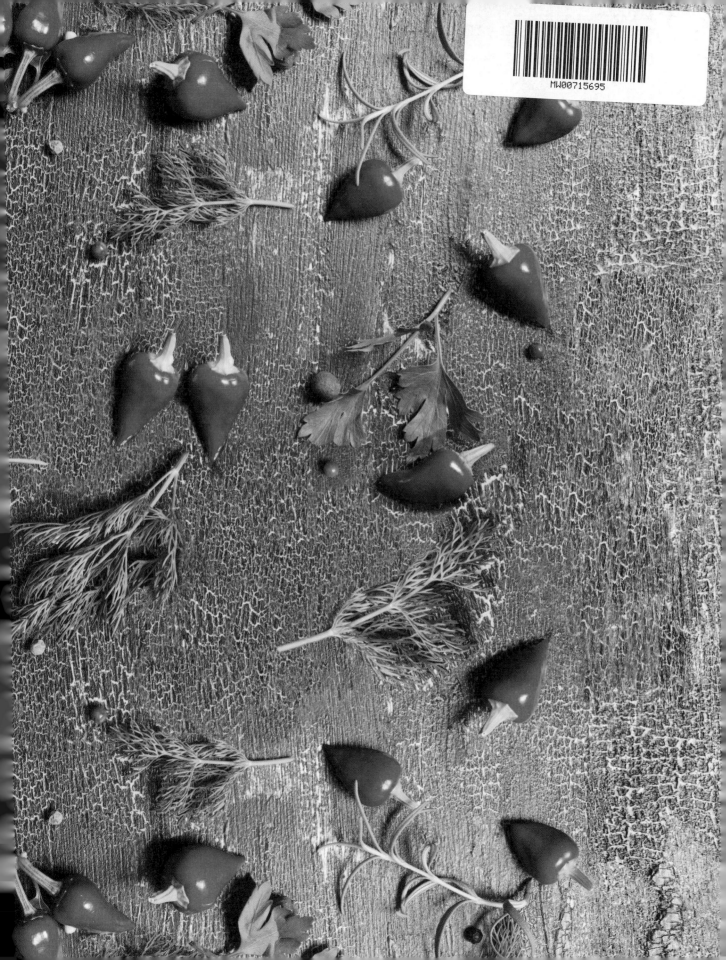

THE ULTIMATE BOOK OF
CHILE
&SPICE

THE ULTIMATE BOOK OF

CHILE & SPICE

100 RECIPES TO HEAT UP
& SPICE UP YOUR LIFE

This edition published by Parragon Books Ltd in 2017 and distributed by

Parragon Inc.
440 Park Avenue South, 13th Floor
New York, NY 10016
www.parragon.com/lovefood

LOVE FOOD is an imprint of Parragon Books Ltd

ISBN 978-1-4748-3809-2

Printed in China

NOTES FOR THE READER

This book uses standard kitchen measuring spoons and cups.
All spoon and cup measurements are level unless otherwise indicated.
Unless otherwise stated, milk is assumed to be whole, eggs are large,
individual vegetables and fruits are medium, pepper is freshly ground
black pepper, and salt is table salt. A pinch of salt is calculated as $\frac{1}{16}$
teaspoon. Unless otherwise stated, all root vegetables should be peeled
prior to using.

The times given are only an approximate guide. Preparation times differ
according to the techniques used by different people, and the cooking
times may also vary from those given.

For best results, use a food thermometer when cooking meat.
Check the latest government guidelines for current advice.

Take care when preparing chiles. The fiery heat comes from the chemical
compound capsaicin, located in the white pithy inner core or rib of the
chile. Capsaicin can aggravate skin and eyes, so always wash your hands
thoroughly after handling chiles. If your skin is sensitive, wear plastic
gloves. Never touch your eyes or mouth after handling chiles without
thoroughly washing your hands first with soap and water.

Front cover recipes, clockwise from top left: p.28 Sticky Bourbon Chicken
Wings; p.46 Spicy Chickpea Red Pepper Soup; p.182 Monkfish & Baby
Broccoli Coconut Soup; p.12 Tabbouleh-Stuffed Jalapeños; p.157 Spiced
Turkey Stew with Whole-Grain Couscous; p.154 Mexican Turkey Burgers
(shown with bell pepper slices); and p.80 Chimichurri Sweltering Sauce.

CONTENTS

CHILES & SPICES
A CULINARY JOURNEY

If you're tired of preparing the same predictable meals and are craving something with a little more oomph, then look no farther. Chile & Spice features 101 sizzling recipes from around the globe to help jazz up your dishes—warming appetizers, snacks and sides; fiery vegetarian, meat, and fish main courses; and tantalizing sweet treats.

SPICES

In ancient times, spices were used to prevent ingredients from spoiling and to disguise food with strong odors and unpleasant flavors. As they became popular for their aromatic flavors, spices were integrated into everyday cuisine, with countries and regions developing their own unique signature dishes based on available indigenous spices. Over time, people discovered the remarkable medicinal properties of specific spices.

Nowadays, we may not give much thought to our ubiquitous, affordable spices as we sprinkle them liberally over ingredients, but they have an incredible history. Once the world's biggest and most dominant industry, the spice trade produced great wealth for many nations. Spices were such precious commodities that nutmeg and pepper were worth more than gold.

The spice trade began with camel caravans in the Middle East some 4,000 years ago. Arabic spice traders spun elaborate myths about how hard the spices were to come by, thereby adding to their allure and driving up prices. The Silk Road connecting Asia with North Africa and Europe played a vital role in building mighty civilizations

and empires, such as those of China, India, Egypt, Persia, Arabia, and Rome.

For centuries, Middle Eastern and North African traders monopolized the spice trade, becoming increasingly wealthy and powerful, and forcing European merchants to pay excessively high prices. By the 1400s, even the nobility was struggling to pay for aromatic luxuries, so explorers were dispatched overseas in search of alternative trade routes.

First to cross the Atlantic Ocean was the Italian explorer Christopher Columbus, who accidentally stumbled across the Americas in 1492 while looking for precious black pepper and a more direct route to India. He discovered new fruit and vegetables, including corn, potatoes, pumpkins, pineapple, avocados, and papayas, and perhaps most notably the much-loved chile pepper.

In 1497, Portuguese explorer Vasco de Gama became the first to sail directly from Africa to India. His sea route around Africa opened up a trade between Europe and Asia, and it resulted in a Portuguese dominance of the spice trade that endured for centuries.

As spice cultivation began to spread around the world, availability became more widespread and prices fell. Highly valuable spices, such as pepper, cinnamon, and nutmeg, are no longer the precious products they once were, but they are just as popular today, still cherished for their vibrant colous, pungent flavors, and enticing aromas.

CHILES

Chile peppers are the pods of perennial, woody-stemmed shrubs that belong to the *Capsicum* genus. They originate from Central America, where archeologists have found traces of their consumption by humans dating back to 7500 BCE. Chiles have been used as a primary ingredient in Mexican cooking for hundreds of years.

Although chile peppers were unheard of in Europe until Columbus's fifteen-century discovery, they had already played a major part in Asian cuisine for some 2,000 years. With the increase in shipping during the sixteenth and seventeenth centuries, Indian and Chinese flavorings spread around the globe. Chiles soon became a favorite way to add piquancy to cooking, especially because they were much cheaper than pepper.

Chiles have never fallen out of favor, and today around 25 percent of the world's population enjoy them in their daily diet. There is a huge variety to choose from, including Thai, Scotch bonnet, habanero, and jalapeño. They are grown widely in many parts of the world as an important commercial crop, but India is the biggest cultivator, exporter, and consumer of this hot pod.

As well as their fiery flavors, chiles also have many nutritional and health-boosting benefits. The pod's heat-emitting chemical compound, capsaicin, has antibacterial, anticarcinogenic, and pain-relieving properties, and may also lower bad cholesterol. Fresh red and green chiles are a rich source of vitamins A, B, and C, as well as minerals such as iron, potassium, magnesium, and copper.

Chiles can be bought fresh, dried, or powdered. Fresh varieties come in vibrant colors of red, green, orange, and yellow, and you should look for firm, plump ones with healthy stems. Avoid buying chiles that are soft, discolored, missing their caps or have spots or signs of mold. Store them in the refrigerator or a cool, dark place for up to two weeks, then wash before use. The most flavorful dried chile peppers are the sun-dried variety. Look for ones with smooth, unblemished skins with a slight bendiness to them. Use within a year.

SPICES IN COOKING

Spices comprise all the dried parts, except the leaves, of a tropical plant or tree, such as the seeds, bark, roots, and berries. Popular spices, which are used to enrich the flavors of culinary ingredients, include mustard, pepper, paprika, cloves, caraway seeds, cinnamon, ginger, and nutmeg, to name just a few of them.

As well as their appealing aromatic properties, many spices are renowned for their healing attributes. For example, turmeric is thought to be an excellent anti-inflammatory. Cloves aid digestion and have antibacterial properties, while ginger helps stave off nausea.

Spices may be dry-fried in a hot wok or saucepan or ground first with a mortar and pestle, then mixed into a paste with a little water. Once spices are ground, their flavor does begin to deteriorate, so

it's preferable if you can grind your own—using a mortar and pestle or coffee grinder—immediately before cooking for optimum flavor. If this is not possible, store bought ground spices in a cool place and use within six months of purchase.

CHILE PREPARATION

To decide whether a chile is mild or hot, first examine its shape. Milder chiles tend to have broader shoulders and blunter tips, whereas hotter ones have narrower shoulders and more pointy tips. Chiles of the same variety can vary in heat intensity. To test before adding to your recipe, try halving the chile and hold it just under your nose. If you feel a buzz, then you know it's a hot one.

Be careful when preparing chiles. The fiery heat comes from the chemical compound capsaicin,

which is located in the white pithy inner core or rib of the chile. Contrary to popular belief, the seeds don't actually contain any heat, but, because they lie close to the pith, they may acquire a layer of the hot compound. Capsaicin can aggravate skin and eyes so it is important to wash hands thoroughly after handling. If you want to reduce the intensity of a chile's heat, then remove the pith and seeds. If it is still too hot to handle, then you can try stirring in some yogurt, sour cream, or ghee to help take it down a notch.

We hope you enjoy your chile and spice journey. On the pages that follow. You will find an impressive range of recipes with the characteristic tastes and flavors of many different types of chiles and spices, from the spices star anise and nutmeg to jalapeño and Scotch bonnet chiles.

APPETIZERS & SNACKS

Prepare to tantalize your taste buds with this enticing selection of piquant hors d'oeuvres and nibbles. The mouthwatering flavors include hot Tabbouleh-Stuffed Jalapeños, Grilled Harissa Shrimp Skewers, Little Curried Crab Cakes, Ultimate Nachos with Beef, protein-packed Spice-Roasted Edamame & Cranberries, and the finger-lickingly addictive Five-Spice Cashew Nuts.

TABBOULEH-STUFFED JALAPEÑOS

| MAKES: 48 | PREP TIME: 22 mins | COOK TIME: 10–12 mins |

JALAPEÑO PEPPERS ARE SMALL IN SIZE BUT CAN PACK A PUNCH WITH FLAVOR AND NUTRITION. PART OF THE NIGHTSHADE FAMILY, THESE LITTLE PEPPERS DERIVE THEIR HEAT FROM A NATURAL COMPOUND CALLED CAPSAICIN, KNOWN TO OFFER POWERFUL HEALTH BENEFITS.

INGREDIENTS

⅓ cup quinoa

2 cups chopped fresh parsley

2½ cups chopped fresh mint

2½ cups chopped fresh cilantro

1 preserved lemon, chopped

1 tablespoon chopped walnuts

seeds from 1 pomegranate

24 jalapeño chiles, halved and seeded

2 avocados, peeled, pitted, and sliced

juice of 1 lemon

salt and pepper (optional)

1. To make the tabbouleh, cook the quinoa according to the package directions. Drain and refresh under cold water, then drain again. Put into a large bowl.

2. Add the parsley, mint, cilantro, preserved lemon, walnuts, and pomegranate seeds and mix thoroughly. Season with salt and pepper, if using.

3. Spoon the tabbouleh into the jalapeños. Top each one with a couple of slices of avocado, then squeeze the lemon juice over them to serve.

VARIATION

FOR A DIFFERENT TOPPING, TRY A TABLESPOON OF HUMMUS SPRINKLED WITH TOASTED SUNFLOWER SEEDS AND SMOKED PAPRIKA.

VEGETABLE SAMOSAS

| MAKES: 14 | PREP TIME: 40–45 mins, plus resting | COOK TIME: 1 hr |

IT TAKES A LITTLE PRACTICE TO MASTER SHAPING THESE INDIAN PASTRIES. MAKE SURE YOU SIMMER THE FILLING MIXTURE UNTIL IT IS DRY BEFORE USING.

INGREDIENTS

2 cups all-purpose flour

½ teaspoon salt

1½ tablespoons clarified butter or butter

1½ teaspoons lemon juice

⅓–½ cup cold water

1 tablespoon butter, for greasing

vegetable or peanut oil, for deep-frying

FILLING

¼ cup clarified butter, vegetable oil, or peanut oil

1 onion, minced

2 garlic cloves, crushed

1 potato, finely diced

2 carrots, finely chopped

2 teaspoons mild, medium, or hot curry powder, to taste

1½ teaspoons ground coriander

1 teaspoon ground turmeric

1 fresh green chile, seeded and finely chopped

1 teaspoon salt

½ teaspoon black mustard seeds

1¼ cups cold water

⅔ cup frozen peas

⅓ cup finely chopped cauliflower florets

1. To make the filling, put the butter into a large skillet over medium–high heat. Add the onion and garlic and sauté for 5–8 minutes, until soft. Stir in the potato and carrots and cook for 5 minutes. Stir in the spices, chile, salt, and mustard seeds. Pour in the water and bring to a boil. Reduce the heat to low and simmer, uncovered, for about 15 minutes. Add the peas and cauliflower and simmer until the vegetables are tender and the liquid has evaporated. Remove from the heat and set aside.

2. Meanwhile, sift the flour and salt into a bowl. Make a well in the center, add the butter or oil and lemon juice, and work them into the flour. Gradually add the water until the mixture comes together to form a soft dough and knead for about 10 minutes, until smooth. Shape into a ball, cover with a damp dish towel, and let rest for 15 minutes.

3. Divide the dough into seven pieces. On a lightly greased work surface, roll each piece of dough into an 8-inch circle, then cut in half to make two semicircles. Keep the remaining pieces of dough covered.

4. Working with one semicircle at a time, wet the edges with water. Place 2 teaspoons of filling on the dough, just off-center. Fold one side into the center, covering the filling. Fold the other side in the opposite direction, overlapping the first fold to form a cone shape. Wet the open edge with water and press to seal.

5. Heat the oil for deep-frying in a saucepan or deep fryer until it reaches 350–375°F. Working in batches, deep-fry the samosas for 2–3 minutes, flipping them over once, until golden brown. Remove with a slotted spoon and drain well on paper towels. Serve warm or at room temperature.

SPICY ONION FRITTERS

SERVES: 4	PREP TIME: 10–15 mins	COOK TIME: 25–30 mins

THESE SERIOUSLY TASTY, SPICED ONION FRITTERS ARE EXTREMELY DIFFICULT TO RESIST! THEY ARE A POPULAR STREET SNACK ALL OVER INDIA AND ARE BEST ENJOYED WITH CHUTNEY FOR DIPPING.

INGREDIENTS

1½ cups chickpea (besan) flour

1 teaspoon salt, or to taste

small pinch of baking soda

2½ tablespoons rice flour

1 teaspoon fennel seeds

1 teaspoon cumin seeds

2 fresh green chiles, finely chopped (seeded if you like)

2 large onions, sliced into semicricles and separated

⅓ cup finely chopped fresh cilantro (both leaves and stems)

1 cup cold water

vegetable oil or peanut oil, for deep-frying

1. Sift the chickpea flour into a large bowl and add the salt, baking soda, rice flour, fennel seeds, and cumin seeds. Mix together well, then add the chiles, onions, and cilantro. Gradually pour in the water and mix until a thick batter is formed and the onions are thoroughly coated with it.

2. Heat enough oil for deep-frying in a large saucepan or deep fryer to 350–375°F, or until a cube of bread browns in 30 seconds. Add as many small amounts (each about 1½ teaspoons) of the batter as will fit in a single layer, without overcrowding the pan. Reduce the heat slightly and cook the fritters for 8–10 minutes, until golden brown and crisp.

3. Use a slotted spoon to remove the fritters from the oil and drain well on paper towels. Continue frying until all the batter mixture has been used. Serve hot.

GRILLED HARISSA SHRIMP SKEWERS

| SERVES: 4 | PREP TIME: 20 mins, plus 30 mins marinating | COOK TIME: 4–6 mins |

THESE HOT, TUNISIAN-INSPIRED SHRIMP SKEWERS ARE GREAT AS PART OF A SHARING PLATTER OR AS AN APPETIZER. YOU WILL NEED FOUR WOODEN SKEWERS.

INGREDIENTS

8 ounces raw jumbo shrimp, peeled and deveined, thawed if frozen

2 teaspoons rose harissa

1 teaspoon fine sea salt

2 garlic cloves, finely chopped

¼ cup finely chopped fresh cilantro

2 tablespoons olive oil

pinch of sea salt flakes

1 lemon, cut into wedges, to serve

1. Mix together the shrimp, rose harissa, fine sea salt, garlic, and half the cilantro in a large bowl. Cover and marinate in the refrigerator for 30 minutes.

2. Soak four wooden skewers in water for 20 minutes, then drain well. Thread the shrimp onto the skewers and brush them lightly with the oil.

3. Heat a ridged grill pan or heavy skillet over high heat until smoking hot. Lay the skewers on the pan, reduce the heat slightly, and cook for 4–6 minutes, or until pink and cooked through, turning halfway.

4. Serve the skewers immediately, sprinkled with the remaining cilantro and the sea salt flakes, with lemon wedges for squeezing over them.

LITTLE CURRIED CRAB CAKES WITH AVOCADO SALAD

MAKES: 8	PREP TIME: 20 mins	COOK TIME: 8 mins

ONCE YOU'VE DONE THE PREPARATION, THESE LITTLE CRAB CAKES ARE EASY TO PUT TOGETHER, AND THEY ARE PERFECTLY COMPLEMENTED BY THE TANGY, CHILE-INFUSED AVOCADO SALAD.

INGREDIENTS

10½ ounces white crabmeat

1 cup drained canned corn kernels

1 cup whole-wheat panko bread crumbs

1 extra-large egg, beaten

1½ tablespoons light mayonnaise

1½ tablespoons fat-free Greek-style yogurt

2 tablespoons snipped fresh chives

2 teaspoons Dijon mustard

1 teaspoon curry powder

¼ teaspoon pepper

10 sprays cooking spray, for oiling

SALAD

1 large ripe avocado

1 tomato, finely chopped

juice of ½ lime

small bunch of fresh cilantro, leaves only

½ fresh red jalapeño chile, seeded and finely chopped

3 scallions, chopped

1. Mix together the crabmeat, corn, bread crumbs, egg, mayonnaise, yogurt, chives, mustard, curry powder, and pepper in a bowl.

2. Using your hands, shape the mixture into eight patties. Spray a nonstick skillet with cooking spray to coat, then heat to just below medium-hot and add the patties to the pan. Cook the patties for 4 minutes, without turning or moving them.

3. Meanwhile, make the salad. Pit, peel, and slice the avocado, then lightly crush it in a bowl. Add the tomato, lime juice, cilantro leaves, chile, and scallions, and stir to combine.

4. Spray the tops of the patties with more cooking spray, then use a metal spatula to turn each one over carefully. Cook for an additional 3 minutes, or until the crab cakes are golden and piping hot. Serve immediately, topped with the avocado salad.

CHILE PEPPERS & THE SCOVILLE SCALE

Chile peppers are a small variety of Capsicum, a genus of tropical pepper plants distinctive for their heat. Ranging from green and yellow to orange, red, and black, there are more than 200 varieties.

The oil that creates the heat in chiles is called *capsaicin*. The amount of this oil in individual chiles can vary dramatically, even within the same chile type. The piquancy or hotness of chile peppers is measured using the Scoville scale, with units measured as SHU. This scale measures how much *capsaicin* is present in a chile. So a sweet pepper scores 0, and a pimento scores 100–1,000, moving right up to the Carolina Reaper at 1,500,000–2,200,000 SHU.

The chiles shown within these pages include the following varieties:

Anaheim peppers are a milder variety of the New Mexico chile pepper. They have a lime-green pod in a long, slender shape and have a mild, sweet, peppery flavor. They measure 500–2,500 SHU.

New Mexico Chiles are green chiles with a flavor that has been likened to an onion, with a subtle hint of sweetness and spiciness. They measure between 800–1,400 SHU on the heat scale.

Cherry Bomb chiles are small, round, and the shape of a cherry. They have a pleasant sweetness and are 2,500–5,000 SHU.

Guajillo chiles, a dried form of the mirasol chile, have a refreshing sweet quality and a tart, fruity flavor and are 2,500–5,000 SHU.

Jalapeño chiles can be used fresh or pickled and can range from moderate to fiery heat, or

2,500–5,000 SHU on the Scoville scale. These chiles are dried and smoked to make chipotles that have a deep, sweet flavor.

Serrano chiles have a substantial heat kick, rating between 8,000 and 23,000 SHU. They are easy to use in salsas because they don't need steaming or peeling before use.

Tabasco chiles are small and hot and have a unique, smoky flavor that is the main contributor to the distinctive taste of Tabasco sauce. They measure 30,000–50,000 SHU.

Thai chiles, also sometimes known as bird's-eye chiles, are small and powerful chiles that measure 50,000–100,000 SHU. They have a spicy, fruity taste and are often used in Southeast Asian cooking.

Habanero chiles have a subtle fruity flavor and measure 100,000–350,000 SHU, so avoid these unless you relish a meal that is blow-your-head-off hot.

Scotch Bonnet chiles, also known as Caribbean red bell peppers, are lantern-shaped red-hot chiles that can be yellow, green, or red. They have a sweeter flavor than habanero and a powerful heat rating of 100,000–350,000 SHU.

Carolina Reaper is currently the world's hottest pepper, measuring 1,500,000–2,200,000 SHU. The chile has a scorpion's tail and a sweet, fruity flavor before the heat hits.

CHIPOTLE TURKEY
CROQUETTES

MAKES: 16	PREP TIME: 35–40 mins	COOK TIME: 20–25 mins

THESE SUPER-HOT CROQUETTES ARE BAKED INSTEAD OF BEING FRIED, AND THE LEAN TURKEY IS PACKED WITH HEALTHY MINERALS, SUCH AS IRON, ZINC, POTASSIUM, AND PHOSPHORUS.

INGREDIENTS

1–2 tablespoons olive oil

4 scallions, quartered

1 small red bell pepper, seeded and cut into chunks

1 carrot, shredded

2 teaspoons fresh thyme leaves

1 pound fresh ground turkey breast

🔥 1 fresh Carolina Reaper chile, minced

1 small dried chipotle chile, finely chopped

1 egg

1 tablespoon cold water

⅓ cup freshly grated Parmesan cheese

½ cup golden flaxseed meal

sea salt and pepper (optional)

AVOCADO DIP

1 large ripe avocado, halved and pitted

grated zest and juice of 1 lime

2 tablespoons fat-free Greek-style yogurt

1. Preheat the oven to 400°F. Brush a baking sheet with a little of the oil and line with parchment paper. Finely chop the scallions and red bell pepper in a food processor. Add the carrot, thyme, and turkey, then sprinkle in the fresh and dried chiles and a little salt and pepper, if using. Process until evenly mixed.

2. Scoop out tablespoons of the mixture onto a cutting board to make 16 oval-shape mounds, then press them into neater shapes between your hands.

3. Lightly mix the egg, water, and a little salt and pepper together in a shallow dish. Mix the cheese and flaxseed in a separate shallow dish. Dip the croquettes, one at a time, into the egg, lift out with two forks, draining well, then roll in the cheese mixture. Place on the prepared baking sheet. Continue until all the croquettes are well coated.

4. Bake in the preheated oven for 20–25 minutes, until golden, turning halfway through cooking and brushing with the remaining oil, if needed. To check that they are cooked, cut one croquette in half—the juices will run clear with no traces of pink.

5. When the croquettes are almost ready to serve, make the dip. Scoop the avocado from the shell, mash with the lime juice and zest, and mix with the yogurt. Spoon into a small bowl set on a large plate, then arrange the hot croquettes around the dish and serve immediately.

STICKY TURKEY KABOBS

SERVES: 2	PREP TIME: 20 mins, plus chilling	COOK TIME: 1 hr 30 mins

THE SOUTHWEST OF TURKEY (THE COUNTRY, OF COURSE) IS WELL KNOWN FOR ITS SPICY KABOBS. HERE, GARLIC, GINGER, AND SOY COMBINE WITH THE PAPRIKA AND CUMIN IN THE SPICY RUB TO GIVE THESE KABOBS A GENTLE KICK.

INGREDIENTS

10 ounces turkey breast meat, cubed

2 cups cooked long-grain rice, to serve

salad greens, to garnish

SPICE RUB
1 tablespoon packed dark brown sugar

¼ teaspoon paprika

¼ teaspoon ground cumin

¼ teaspoon salt

¼ teaspoon pepper

STICKY SAUCE
1 tablespoon vegetable oil

1 onion, finely chopped

2 garlic cloves, finely chopped

1-inch piece ginger, grated

3 tablespoons ketchup

3 tablespoons white wine or apple cider vinegar

3 tablespoons soy sauce

2 tablespoons packed light brown sugar

1 cup water

1. Put the turkey into a bowl and add the spice rub ingredients, mixing well to coat. Chill in the refrigerator for at least 1 hour.

2. Meanwhile, make the sauce. Heat the oil in a saucepan over medium heat, add the onion, garlic, and ginger and cook for 5 minutes. Add the ketchup, wine vinegar, soy sauce, sugar, and water and bring to a boil. Reduce the heat and simmer for 1 hour, stirring regularly, until the mixture is thick and sticky.

3. If using wooden skewers, soak them in water for 30 minutes to prevent them from burning. Preheat the barbecue or broiler to hot. Thread the turkey pieces onto skewers and lay them on a sheet of aluminum foil. Set aside some of the sticky sauce for serving, then brush a little of the sticky sauce on the kabobs. Cook the kabobs on the grill or under the broiler for 10–15 minutes, turning and brushing with more of the sticky sauce until cooked. Serve with the rice and the reserved sticky sauce, garnished with salad greens.

STICKY BOURBON
CHICKEN WINGS

SERVES: 4	PREP TIME: 20 mins	COOK TIME: 20–30 mins

PAPRIKA IS THE KEY SPICE PLAYER HERE, BUT IT HAS THE HELP OF ITS FRIENDS GROUND CUMIN, WORCESTERSHIRE SAUCE, CHIPOTLE PASTE, AND, LAST BUT NOT LEAST, BOURBON. REPLACE THE BOURBON WITH APPLE JUICE IF YOU PREFER.

INGREDIENTS

2¼ pounds chicken wings, tips removed

1 tablespoon vegetable oil, for brushing

RUB
1 tablespoon paprika

½ teaspoon ground cumin

1 teaspoon dried thyme

1 teaspoon dried oregano

1 teaspoon salt

1 teaspoon pepper

BOURBON GLAZE
2 tablespoons bourbon

2 tablespoons apple cider vinegar

1 tablespoon Worcestershire sauce

2 tablespoons molasses

2 tablespoons ketchup

2 tablespoons chipotle paste

1 tablespoon mustard

½ teaspoon salt

½ teaspoon pepper

1. To make the rub, combine all the ingredients in a large bowl.

2. Cut each chicken wing in half. Add the wing pieces to the bowl containing the rub and turn until coated thoroughly.

3. To make the bourbon glaze, put a medium saucepan over medium heat. Add the bourbon and flambé. When the flames have disappeared, add the remaining glaze ingredients and simmer over medium heat until the sauce has reduced by half.

4. Prepare the barbecue grill for direct cooking and preheat to medium-hot.

5. Thread half of the chicken wing pieces onto two metal skewers, creating a raft shape. Repeat with the remaining wings. Brush the wings with the bourbon glaze.

6. Lightly brush the barbecue rack with the oil and cook the wings for 10 minutes on each side, brushing with more glaze as they cook.

7. Cook until the chicken is tender and the juices run clear when the tip of a sharp knife is inserted into the thickest part of the meat. The meat should come away easily from the bone. Remove from the skewers and serve.

MASALA SHRIMP CAKES

MAKES: 20	PREP TIME: 20 mins, plus chilling	COOK TIME: 12–15 minutes

PERFECT AS CANAPÉS, THESE SHRIMP CAKES ARE PACKED WITH THE PUNCHY, FRESH FLAVORS OF GARLIC, GINGER, COCONUT, CHILE, CILANTRO, AND MINT. SQUEEZE A LITTLE LIME JUICE OVER THEM AND SERVE WITH A CHILLED DRINK.

INGREDIENTS

1¾ pounds raw jumbo shrimp, peeled and deveined
2 fresh red chiles, seeded and minced
⅓ cup finely chopped fresh cilantro
⅓ cup finely chopped fresh mint
1 teaspoon coconut cream or coconut milk
4 scallions, finely sliced
2 garlic cloves, finely chopped
2 teaspoon finely grated fresh ginger
½ cup fresh white bread crumbs
2 teaspoons ground cumin
1 teaspoon chili powder
1 medium egg, lightly beaten
¼ cup vegetable oil or peanut oil
lime wedges, to serve

1. Coarsely chop the shrimp and put them into a food processor with the remaining ingredients, apart from the oil. Blend to a coarse paste. Transfer the mixture to a bowl, cover, and chill in the refrigerator for at least 6–8 hours, or overnight.

2. Preheat the oven to 400°F. Line a baking sheet with parchment paper.

3. Shape the fish mixture into 20 small patties, about 1½ inches in diameter. Place on the prepared baking sheet and lightly brush with the oil. Bake in the preheated oven for 12–15 minutes, or until slightly puffed up and light golden.

4. Serve warm or at room temperature with lime wedges for squeezing over.

ULTIMATE NACHOS
WITH BEEF

SERVES: 2	PREP TIME: 10 mins	COOK TIME: 30 mins

WHEN YOU'RE EXPECTING CHILE-LOVERS FOR DINNER, THIS IS A REALLY QUICK AND EASY DISH TO SERVE. THE SAUCE IS SPICY HOT, SO IT WILL KEEP YOUR TONGUE FIRED UP, AND ANY LEFTOVERS MAKE A DELICIOUS TACO FILLING.

INGREDIENTS

2 tablespoons olive oil
1 onion, chopped
8 ounces fresh ground round beef
1 tablespoon dried oregano
1 tablespoon paprika
1 tablespoon ground cumin
1½ cups tomato puree or tomato sauce
1 cup water
2 tablespoons butter
¼ cup all-purpose flour
2 cups milk, warmed
1 cup shredded cheddar cheese,
1 cup shredded Monterey Jack cheese
1 tablespoon mustard
⅔ cup cup grated Parmesan cheese
8 cups tortilla chips
1 ripe avocado
¼ cup drained pickled jalapeños
1 small red onion, finely chopped
salt and pepper (optional)

1. In a medium saucepan, heat the oil over medium–high heat and add the onion. Cook for 5 minutes, or until translucent and slightly golden. Add the meat and cook for an additional 5 minutes, breaking up the meat with a wooden spoon until it starts to brown.

2. Add the oregano, paprika, cumin, tomato puree, and water, and cook over low heat for 20 minutes, or until reduced by half. Season with salt and pepper, if using, and set aside, keeping warm.

3. Meanwhile, melt the butter in a medium saucepan, add the flour, and mix well with a wooden spoon. Slowly add the warm milk, trying to keep any lumps from forming, until the sauce thickens and starts to boil. Turn off the heat and add the cheddar cheese, Monterey Jack cheese, mustard, and half the Parmesan cheese. Stir until smooth, season with salt and pepper, if using, and set aside.

4. Ladle half the cooked beef over a large serving platter. Place the tortilla chips on top, followed by the rest of the meat, then top with the cheese sauce.

5. Cut the avocado in half and remove the pit, then peel and chop into small pieces. Spread the avocado pieces over the nachos along with the jalapeños, chopped red onion, and the remaining Parmesan cheese. Serve immediately.

SPICY OVEN-BAKED COATED EGGS

SERVES: 4	PREP TIME: 25 mins	COOK TIME: 30 mins

THESE SAUSAGE-COATED EGGS ARE PACKED WITH FLAVOR, BUT ARE LOWER IN FAT AND SIMPLER TO PREPARE THAN THE ORIGINAL PICNIC FARE KNOWN AS SCOTCH EGGS, INVENTED BY LONDON DEPARTMENT STORE FORTNUM AND MASON.

INGREDIENTS

4 extra-large eggs

1 tablespoon oil, for oiling

10½ ounces sausages, casings removed

1 tablespoon mild curry paste

1 teaspoon onion seeds

2 tablespoons fresh flat-leaf parsley leaves, coarsely chopped

1 cup fresh white bread crumbs

2 tablespoons milk

tomato relish, to serve

1. Put the eggs into a saucepan and cover with cold water. Bring to a boil, then remove from the heat. Cover the pan and let stand for 6 minutes. Drain and cool under cold running water, then carefully peel off the shells.

2. Preheat the oven to 375°F. Lightly oil a baking sheet or line with nonstick parchment paper. Put the sausage meat, curry paste, onion seeds, and parsley into a bowl. Mix well. Add the bread crumbs and milk and mix again. Divide into four equal portions.

3. Lay a piece of plastic wrap on the work surface. Place one-quarter of the sausage mixture on top and flatten with clean hands to a diameter of about 5 inches. Place an egg in the center and use the plastic wrap to lift and mold the mixture around it. Smooth over the edges to seal. Place on the baking sheet. Repeat with the remaining sausage mixture and eggs.

4. Bake in the preheated oven for 25 minutes, until lightly browned, and serve with chutney.

SPICE-ROASTED EDAMAME & CRANBERRIES

SERVES: 4	PREP TIME: 15 mins	COOK TIME: 15 mins

FROZEN EDAMAME OR YOUNG SOYBEANS MAKE A HEALTHY, PROTEIN-PACKED SNACK, AND THEIR HIGH LEVELS OF FIBER KEEP YOU FEELING FULLER LONGER.

INGREDIENTS

2 cups frozen edamame (soybeans)

2-inch piece fresh ginger, peeled and finely grated

1 teaspoon Sichuan peppercorns, coarsely crushed

1 tablespoon soy sauce

1 tablespoon olive oil

3 small star anise

⅓ cup dried cranberries

1. Preheat the oven to 350°F. Put the beans into a roasting pan, then sprinkle with the ginger and peppercorns, drizzle with soy sauce and oil, and mix together.

2. Tuck the star anise in among the beans, then roast, uncovered, in the preheated oven for 15 minutes.

3. Stir in the cranberries and let cool. Spoon into a small jar and eat within 12 hours.

TIP

EDAMAME BEANS ARE EXTREMELY VERSATILE AND PACK A MUCH GREATER NUTRITIONAL PUNCH THAN FROZEN PEAS.

FIVE-SPICE
CASHEW NUTS

| SERVES: 8 | PREP TIME: 5 mins | COOK TIME: 10–12 mins |

PEPPERCORNS, STAR ANISE, FENNEL, CLOVES, AND CINNAMON COMBINE HERE WITH THE NATURAL SWEETNESS OF CASHEW NUTS. THIS NUTTY CONCOCTION PERFORMS AT EVERY LEVEL, WHETHER FOR A SNACK OR AN APPETIZER.

INGREDIENTS

1 tablespoon peanut oil, for oiling

½ teaspoon Sichuan peppercorns

2 star anise

½ teaspoon fennel seeds

6 whole cloves

½ teaspoon ground cinnamon

2 tablespoons water

¼ cup firmly packed light brown sugar

1 teaspoon salt

2 cups unsalted, toasted cashew nuts

1. Preheat the oven to 400°F. Lightly oil a baking pan and a large piece of aluminum foil.

2. In a spice grinder, grind together the peppercorns, star anise pods, fennel seeds, and cloves until finely ground. Add the cinnamon and mix well.

3. Put the water and sugar into a medium saucepan and heat over medium heat, stirring constantly, for 2 minutes, or until the sugar has dissolved. Add the spice mixture and salt and stir to mix well. Add the nuts and stir to coat completely. Cook, stirring, for an additional minute.

4. Transfer the nuts to the prepared pan and spread out in an even layer. Roast in the preheated oven for 6–8 minutes, until most of the liquid has evaporated. Transfer the nuts to the prepared foil and separate them so that they don't stick together. Let cool completely before serving.

5. Store in an airtight container at room temperature for up to two weeks.

LIGHT MEALS & FAST FARE

Looking for a light lunch or supper? Or a speedy, satisfying solution when you're short of time? Then this warming range of flavorsome recipes should hit the spot. From hearty soups and fresh salads to spicy omelets and tacos, each dish promises to satisfy your appetite. How about Vegetable Noodle Broth, Chile Squid with Watercress or a Spicy Fish Stick Sandwich?

CHICKEN SOUP
WITH CHILE & COUSCOUS

SERVES: 4	PREP TIME: 20 mins	COOK TIME: 1¾ hours

THE BROTH FOR THIS TRADITIONAL MIDDLE EASTERN SOUP IS MADE WITH A WHOLE CHICKEN, WHICH IS THEN TORN INTO STRIPS BEFORE BEING ADDED BACK TO THE SOUP. LEBANESE SEVEN SPICE IS A MIXTURE OFTEN USED IN DISHES WITH GROUND BEEF OR LAMB, AS WELL AS POULTRY.

INGREDIENTS

1 tablespoon olive oil

2 onions, finely chopped

1 red chile, seeded and finely chopped

1 teaspoon ground cumin

1 teaspoon paprika

1 teaspoon granulated sugar

2 teaspoons dried mint

1 tablespoon tomato paste

½ cup couscous

3 tablespoons finely chopped fresh cilantro, to garnish

1 lemon, cut into wedges, to serve

BROTH

1 (3-pound) ready-to-cook chicken

1 onion, quartered

1 unwaxed lemon, quartered

⅓ cup fresh parsley stems

1 teaspoon coriander seeds

1 cinnamon stick

pinch of sea salt

pinch of pepper

1. To make the broth, put the chicken, onion, lemon, parsley stems, coriander seeds, and cinnamon stick into a deep saucepan and pour in just enough water to cover. Bring to a boil, then reduce the heat to medium–low, cover, and simmer for 1 hour, or until the chicken is almost falling off the bone. To check it is cooked, pierce the thickest part of the thigh with the tip of a sharp knife. Any juices should be piping hot and clear with no traces of red or pink.

2. Transfer the chicken to a large plate and let cool slightly. Meanwhile, simmer the broth until it has reduced to about 5 cups. Season with the salt and pepper, then strain into a bowl. Remove the skin from the chicken and tear the flesh into strips.

3. Heat the oil in a heavy saucepan over medium heat. Add the onions and chile and sauté for 2–3 minutes, stirring often. Stir in the cumin, paprika, sugar, mint, and tomato paste, then pour in the broth. Bring to a boil, then gradually stir in the couscous. Reduce the heat to medium–low and simmer for 15 minutes. Stir in the cooked chicken strips and simmer for 5 minutes.

4. Serve the soup in shallow bowls, garnished with the cilantro, with lemon wedges for squeezing over the top.

SPICY LENTIL &
CARROT SOUP

| SERVES: 4 | PREP TIME: 15 mins | COOK TIME: 45–50 mins |

RED LENTILS ARE NOT ONLY A GOOD SOURCE OF PROTEIN BUT ALSO THE PERFECT VESSEL FOR ABSORBING STRONG, SPICY FLAVORS.

INGREDIENTS

⅔ cup red lentils

5 cups vegetable broth or stock

6 carrots, sliced

2 onions, chopped

1 cup canned diced tomatoes

2 garlic cloves, chopped

2 tablespoons oil

1 teaspoon ground cumin

1 teaspoon ground coriander

1 fresh green chile, seeded and chopped

½ teaspoon ground turmeric

1 tablespoon lemon juice

1¼ cups milk

2 tablespoons chopped fresh cilantro

salt and pepper (optional)

TO SERVE

4 teaspoons plain yogurt

naan or other flatbread

spicy poppadums

1. Put the lentils into a large saucepan, together with 3¾ cups of the broth or stock, the carrots, onions, tomatoes, and garlic. Bring the mixture to a boil, then reduce the heat, cover, and simmer for 30 minutes, or until the vegetables and lentils are tender.

2. Meanwhile, heat the oil in a separate saucepan. Add the cumin, ground coriander, chile, and turmeric and cook over low heat for 1 minute. Remove from the heat and stir in the lemon juice. Season with salt, if using.

3. Remove the soup from the heat and let cool slightly. Transfer to a food processor or blender, in batches if necessary, and process until smooth. Return the soup to the rinsed-out pan, add the spice mixture and the remaining broth or stock, and simmer over low heat for 10 minutes.

4. Add the milk, taste, and adjust the seasoning, adding salt and pepper if using. Stir in the chopped cilantro and reheat gently; do not boil. Ladle into warm bowls and serve immediately with yogurt, naan, and spicy poppadums.

SPICY CHICKPEA
RED PEPPER SOUP

SERVES: 4	PREP TIME: 15 mins	COOK TIME: 25 mins

CHICKPEAS HAVE BEEN SHOWN TO HELP REGULATE BLOOD SUGAR AND IMPROVE SATIETY AFTER A MEAL, MAKING THEM A USEFUL INGREDIENT IN THIS TASTY SOUP.

INGREDIENTS

2½ tablespoons olive oil

6 scallions, chopped

1 large fresh red jalapeño chile, seeded and finely sliced

4 garlic cloves, finely chopped

2 teaspoons ground cumin

1 teaspoon chili powder

3 fresh ripe tomatoes, peeled and coarsely chopped

2¼ cups drained and thinly sliced roasted red peppers in water

1 tablespoon red pepper pesto

4 cups reduced-sodium vegetable broth or stock

2½ cups drained and rinsed, canned chickpeas

1 teaspoon stevia granules

2 teaspoons red wine vinegar

3½ cups baby spinach leaves

pepper (optional)

4 thick slices bread, to serve

1. Heat the oil in a large saucepan over medium heat. Add the scallions and cook for 2–3 minutes, stirring occasionally, until soft.

2. Add the chile, garlic, cumin, and chili powder and cook for 1 minute, stirring.

3. Stir in the tomatoes, roasted red peppers, pesto, and broth or stock and bring to a simmer. Cook for 10 minutes, then add the chickpeas, stevia granules, vinegar, and pepper, if using, and cook for an additional 5 minutes.

4. Stir in the spinach and cook for 1 minute, until the spinach wilts. Serve with bread.

VEGETABLE NOODLE BROTH

SERVES: 4	PREP TIME: 25–30 mins	COOK TIME: 25–30 minutes

THIS HEARTY VEGETARIAN VERSION OF A POPULAR NOODLE-BASED BROTH IS A GOOD EXAMPLE OF THE INFLUENCE OF TIBETAN CUISINE IN THE BENGAL REGION. THE BROTH IS A GREAT FAVORITE WITH STUDENTS.

INGREDIENTS

16 ounces dried thick egg noodles

2 tablespoons vegetable oil or peanut oil

1 onion, finely chopped

1 teaspoon ground cumin

½ teaspoon ground turmeric

2 garlic cloves, crushed

2 teaspoons grated fresh ginger

1 teaspoon salt

2 fresh green chiles, finely chopped

1 cup thinly sliced snow peas (sliced lengthwise)

2 large carrots, cut into matchsticks

1 red bell pepper, seeded and thinly sliced

2 tomatoes, finely chopped

2 tablespoons dark soy sauce

4 cups vegetable broth

1 teaspoon pepper

7 cups baby spinach leaves

⅓ cup finely chopped fresh cilantro

1 teaspoon toasted sesame oil

1. Cook the noodles according to the package directions. Drain, rinse with cold water, and set aside.

2. Meanwhile, heat the vegetable oil in a large saucepan over medium heat. Add the onion, and sauté for 8–10 minutes, or until lightly browned.

3. Add the cumin, turmeric, garlic, ginger, salt, and chiles to the pan and cook for 1–2 minutes. Add the snow peas, carrots, and red bell pepper and sauté for an additional 1–2 minutes.

4. Add the tomatoes, soy sauce, broth, and pepper. Bring to a boil, then reduce the heat and simmer for 10–12 minutes, until the vegetables are tender.

5. Add the reserved noodles and the spinach and bring back to a boil. Stir until the spinach wilts, then remove from the heat and stir in the chopped cilantro and sesame oil. Ladle into bowls and serve immediately.

HOT & SOUR
ZUCCHINI

SERVES: 4	PREP TIME: 15 mins, plus draining	COOK TIME: 5 mins

THIS SIMPLE DISH HAS A MEDIUM-HOT PUNCH OF TASTY APACHE CHILE. THE ZUCCHINI CAN BE PREPARED AS A VEGETABLE SIDE SERVING OR AS A DELICIOUS LIGHT SNACK WITH CRUSTY BREAD OR SESAME NOODLES.

INGREDIENTS

2 large zucchini, thinly sliced

1 teaspoon salt

2 tablespoons peanut oil

1 teaspoon Sichuan peppercorns, crushed

1 red Apache chile, seeded and sliced into thin strips

1 large garlic clove, thinly sliced

½ teaspoon finely chopped fresh ginger

1 tablespoon rice vinegar

1 tablespoon light soy sauce

2 teaspoons sugar

1 scallion, green part included, thinly sliced

a few drops of sesame oil, to garnish

1 teaspoon sesame seeds, to garnish

1. Put the zucchini slices into a large colander and toss with the salt. Cover with a plate and put a weight on top. Let drain for 20 minutes. Rinse off the salt and spread out the slices on paper towels to dry.

2. Preheat a wok over high heat and add the peanut oil. Add the peppercorns, chile, garlic, and ginger. Cook for about 20 seconds, until the garlic is just beginning to brown.

3. Add the zucchini slices and toss in the oil. Add the rice vinegar, soy sauce, and sugar and stir-fry for 2 minutes. Add the scallion and cook for 30 seconds. Garnish with the sesame oil and sesame seeds and serve immediately.

PREPARING CHILES

Chiles, especially the hotter ones, need to be handled carefully because the capsaicin, which creates the heat, is an irritant. Soak or toast chiles to enhance their flavor and make them easier to use.

Managing chile heat

It is the capsaicin in a chile that provides the heat and, as a rule, the smaller and thinner a chile is, the hotter it will taste. A chile's capsaicin is produced in a gland running down the middle of the fruit and this is the hottest part, although the seeds themselves are not that hot. If you seed the chile and remove the membrane, you can reduce the heat.

Capsaicin is an oil and will stick to your skin, so be careful when chopping chiles, especially if you are removing the gland or the seeds. If your skin is sensitive, wear plastic gloves and never touch your eyes or mouth after handling chiles without first thoroughly washing your hands with soap and water. You can also protect your hands by first rubbing them with vegetable oil, which acts as an effective barrier.

Pan-frying chiles can release a potent vapor that may irritate your eyes, so set the extractor fan to high before starting, or open a window.

If the heat of a chile is too much in your mouth, don't drink a glass of water, which spreads the heat around. Reach, instead, for milk or yogurt, because dairy helps to dilute the heat more effectively.

Toasting chiles

Toasting both fresh and dried chiles endows them with a depth of flavor that will create a much richer final dish. To toast chiles, cook them in a dry skillet over medium heat until you can smell their aroma. Press large chiles, such as guajillos and pasillas, with a metal spatula against the hot surface until they puff up and soften. Smaller chiles, such as pequin, should be stirred constantly so they don't burn. You want blackened and blistered skins, but don't over-toast them or they will taste bitter. Immediately remove them from the pan and set aside.

Another technique is to put the chiles on a baking sheet in an oven, preheated to 425°F, for 5 minutes, or until the chiles slightly puff up and soften.

Soaking chiles

Many recipes specify soaking chiles so they are soft enough to blend. This can mean softening fresh chiles or rehydrating dried ones. You can do this by putting the chiles into a heatproof bowl and pouring over enough boiling water to cover. Let stand for 5 minutes, until the chiles are softened and flexible. Smaller chiles, such as Thai and chipotle, will need to be weighed down with a small saucepan lid or heatproof plate to keep them submerged. Strain the chiles well, then pat dry and remove the stems. If you want to reduce the heat of the chiles, seed and remove the membrane before soaking them.

Never throw away the liquid you soak your chiles in. It is full of flavor and is great for giving a kick to soups, stews, and gravies. Let it cool, then transfer to an airtight container and store in the refrigerator. Or for the especially organized, freeze in an ice-cube tray, then transfer the individual cubes to a freezer-proof bag.

CHILE SQUID
WITH WATERCRESS

| SERVES: 4 | PREP TIME: 4 mins, plus chilling | COOK TIME: 4 minutes |

HERE IS A SALAD THAT IS BOTH COOL AND HOT, CONSISTING OF FRESH SALAD GREENS, STIR-FRIED SQUID, AND EXTRA-HOT THAI CHILES.

INGREDIENTS

12 squid tubes and tentacles (about 1½ pounds), cleaned and prepared

2–3 tablespoons olive oil

2 Thai red chiles, seeded and thinly sliced

2 scallions, finely chopped

lemon wedges, for squeezing, plus extra to serve

3 handfuls of watercress

2 handfuls of baby spinach or arugula

freshly ground black pepper (optional)

DRESSING

½ cup olive oil

juice of a lime

2 shallots, thinly sliced

1 medium tomato, peeled, seeded, and finely chopped

1 garlic clove, crushed

freshly ground black pepper

1. To make the dressing, mix the oil, lime juice, shallots, tomato, and garlic together in a bowl, season with pepper, then cover and refrigerate until required.

2. Cut the squid tubes into 2-inch pieces, then lightly score diamond patterns across the flesh with the tip of a sharp knife. Heat the oil in a wok or large skillet over high heat, add the squid pieces and tentacles, and stir-fry for 1 minute. Add the chiles and scallions and stir-fry for an additional minute. Season with pepper, if using, and add a good squeeze of lemon juice.

3. Mix the watercress and spinach together, then toss with enough of the dressing to coat lightly. Serve immediately with the squid, together with lemon wedges to squeeze over the dish.

TIP

IF YOU CAN, CHOOSE FRESH, OPEN BUNCHES OF WATERCRESS INSTEAD OF THOSE THAT ARE PACKAGED IN SEALED BAGS.

EGGPLANT
PAPRIKA SALAD

SERVES: 4	PREP TIME: 15 mins	COOK TIME: 20 mins

THIS WARM SALAD IS A SATISFYING WAY TO EAT EGGPLANTS, BRINGING YOU SMOKY FLAVORS, A VARIETY OF TEXTURES, AND WARMING SPICES, ALTOGETHER ON THE SAME PLATE.

INGREDIENTS

2 eggplants

2 tablespoons olive oil

2 red bell peppers, seeded and cut into 6 pieces each

2½ cups drained and rinsed, canned chickpeas

1 red onion, finely chopped

4 whole-wheat pita breads, to serve

DRESSING

3 tablespoons olive oil

juice of ½ lemon

1 teaspoon ground coriander

1 teaspoon ground cumin

2 teaspoons smoked paprika

1 teaspoon sugar

small bunch of fresh cilantro, leaves removed and reserved and stems chopped

salt and pepper (optional)

1. Preheat the broiler to high. Cut the eggplants lengthwise into ½-inch-thick slices, brush with oil on both sides, and arrange on a broiler rack. Add the red bell pepper pieces. Cook under the preheated broiler until the eggplants are charred in patches on the top side; turn over and cook until the eggplants are soft and the red bell pepper pieces are lightly cooked and slightly brown in places. Remove from the heat but do not turn off the broiler. Cut the eggplant slices into large bite-size pieces and put into a shallow serving dish with the red bell pepper pieces, chickpeas, and red onion.

2. To make the dressing, combine the oil, lemon juice, ground coriander, cumin, paprika, and sugar with salt and pepper, if using, in a small bowl. Add the cilantro stems to the dressing and stir to combine. Spoon the dressing evenly over the salad and stir—it's best to do this while the vegetables are still warm.

3. Meanwhile, lightly toast the pita breads under the broiler.

4. Sprinkle the salad with the reserved cilantro leaves and serve with the pita breads.

SHAKSHUKA EGGS
WITH SPICY TOMATO SAUCE

SERVES: 4	PREP TIME: 10 mins	COOK TIME: 35 mins

ORIGINATING IN NORTH AFRICA, SHAKSHUKA IS A WARMING AND DELICIOUS BREAKFAST DISH. IT IS DELICIOUS SERVED WITH A HUNK OF CRUSTY BREAD TO HELP MOP UP THE JUICES.

INGREDIENTS

1 teaspoon cumin seeds
1 teaspoon coriander seeds
2 teaspoons olive oil
1 onion, finely chopped
4 cups canned plum tomatoes
¼ cup chile pesto
pinch of saffron
¼ teaspoon cayenne pepper
½ teaspoon salt
1 teaspoon pepper
3 tablespoons chopped fresh cilantro
4 extra-large eggs

1. Crush the cumin seeds and coriander seeds. Put a nonstick skillet over medium heat and add the seeds to the pan. Stir for 1 minute, or until their aromas are released.

2. Reduce the heat to medium-low, add the oil, and heat. Add the onion and cook, stirring occasionally, for 5 minutes, or until the onion is soft and just turning slightly golden.

3. Add the tomatoes, breaking up any large ones, pesto, saffron, cayenne pepper, and salt and pepper. Stir well, bring to a simmer, and cook for 15 minutes, adding a little hot water toward the end if the pan looks too dry (but you don't want the sauce to be too runny). Stir in half of the fresh cilantro.

4. Make four wells in the sauce and break an egg into each one. Cover the pan and cook over low heat for 10 minutes, or until the egg whites are set but the yolk is still runny. Sprinkle the remaining fresh cilantro over the top and serve immediately.

AVOCADO, BACON &
CHILE FRITTATA

| SERVES: 4 | PREP TIME: 15 mins | COOK TIME: 14 mins |

INSPIRED BY THE MEXICAN FLAVORS OF CHILES AND AVOCADO, THIS PROTEIN-PACKED FRITTATA IS WONDERFUL LINGERED OVER ON A LAZY MORNING. YOU CAN MAKE IT AHEAD AND STORE IT IN THE REFRIGERATOR FOR TWO DAYS.

INGREDIENTS

1 tablespoon vegetable oil

8 bacon strips, coarsely chopped

6 eggs, beaten

3 tablespoons heavy cream

2 large avocados, peeled, pitted, and sliced

1 fresh red Mexican poblano chile (or, for a hotter option, 1 serrano), seeded and thinly sliced

½ lime

sea salt and pepper (optional)

1. Preheat the broiler to medium. Heat the oil in an 8-inch ovenproof skillet over medium heat. Add the bacon and cook, stirring, for 4–5 minutes, or until crisp and golden. Using a slotted spoon, transfer to a plate lined with paper towels. Remove the pan from the heat.

2. Pour the eggs into a bowl, add the cream, and season with salt and pepper, if using, then beat. Return the pan to the heat. When it is hot, pour in the egg mixture and cook for 1–2 minutes, without stirring. Sprinkle the bacon and avocado on top and cook for an additional 2–3 minutes, or until the frittata is almost set and the underside is golden brown.

3. Put the frittata under the broiler and cook for 3–4 minutes, or until the top is golden brown and the egg is set. Sprinkle with the chile and squeeze the juice of the lime half over the top. Cut into wedges and serve.

TIP

THE SOFT TEXTURE OF THE FRITTATA WORKS BEST WITH REALLY CRISPY BACON, SO COOK THE BACON OVER MEDIUM HEAT UNTIL IT HAS A DARK GOLDEN COLOR.

EGG WHITE OMELET
WITH SPICY FILLING

| SERVES: 1 | PREP TIME: 10 mins | COOK TIME: 10 mins |

RICH IN PROTEIN AND FIBER, AN EGG WHITE OMELET IS AN EASY AND SATISFYING LUNCH, ESPECIALLY WHEN STUFFED WITH A TASTY, SPICY FILLING.

INGREDIENTS

4 egg whites

¼ teaspoon salt

1 tablespoon water

2 teaspoons oil from a jar of semi-dried tomatoes

2 scallions, finely chopped

⅓ cup rinsed, canned mixed beans, such as kidney beans, pinto beans, and black-eyed peas

¼ cup frozen corn kernels, thawed

¼ cup hot tomato salsa

3 semi-dried tomatoes in oil, drained and chopped

½ teaspoon smoked paprika

½ teaspoon pepper

2 tablespoons chopped fresh cilantro

5 sprays cooking oil spray

1. Put the egg whites into a bowl with the salt and water and beat together.

2. Put the oil into a small skillet over medium heat. Add the scallion and sauté for 1 minute, until soft.

3. Add the beans and corn to the pan with the tomato salsa, tomatoes, paprika, and pepper. Cook for a few minutes, then stir in half of the cilantro. Set the mixture aside and keep warm.

4. Spray a separate small skillet with the cooking oil spray and heat over high heat until hot. Pour in the egg white mixture and cook, making sure that the egg cooks evenly. When the underside is golden and the top is cooked but still moist, spoon the bean filling over the top, then sprinkle over the remaining chopped cilantro.

5. Tip the pan gently to one side, fold the omelet in half, and slide out onto a warm serving plate. Serve immediately.

STUFFED CHILE BHAJIS

| MAKES: 8 | PREP TIME: 20 mins, plus soaking | COOK TIME: 10 mins |

THIS SNACK OF CHILES STUFFED WITH A SPICED POTATO MIXTURE IS A CENTRAL INDIAN SPECIALTY, AND IS TRADITIONAL STREET FOOD. SERVE IT WITH YOUR FAVORITE CHUTNEY OR PLAIN YOGURT.

INGREDIENTS

8 large, mild fresh green chiles

vegetable oil or peanut oil, for deep-frying batter

2¾ cups chickpea (besan) flour

¾ cup rice flour

½ teaspoon baking powder

1 teaspoon ground cumin

2 teaspoons salt

1 teaspoon chili powder

about 3 cups cold water

STUFFING

2 tablespoons vegetable oil or peanut oil

1 teaspoon fennel seeds

2 teaspoons black mustard seeds

1 teaspoon cumin seeds

1 potato, peeled, boiled, and mashed

3 tablespoons finely chopped fresh cilantro

1 teaspoon salt

½ teaspoon tamarind paste

1 tablespoon roasted peanuts, coarsely chopped

1. Halve the chiles lengthwise and remove all the seeds, using a small teaspoon. Soak the chiles in boiling water for 5 minutes. Drain on paper towels and set aside.

2. Mix together the batter ingredients with enough of the water to make a thin batter with the consistency of heavy cream. Set aside.

3. To make the stuffing, heat the oil in a saucepan. Add the fennel seeds, mustard seeds, and cumin seeds. When the seeds start to pop, add the potato, cilantro, and salt and mix well. Add the tamarind paste and sprinkle the roasted peanuts over the potato mixture. Remove from the heat and mash until evenly combined.

4. Using your fingers, stuff the green chiles with the potato mixture.

5. Heat enough oil for deep-frying in a large saucepan or deep fryer to 350–375°F, or until a cube of bread browns in 30 seconds. Working in batches, dip the stuffed green chiles in the batter and deep-fry for 2–3 minutes, or until crisp and golden. Remove with a slotted spoon and drain on paper towels. Serve warm.

SPICY FISH STICK
SANDWICH

SERVES: 2	PREP TIME: 10 mins	COOK TIME: 10 mins

FOR AN INSTANT SPICY SNACK, PREPARE SOME STANDARD FISH STICKS, THEN FLAVOR THEM WITH A RUSSIAN DRESSING THAT HAS CREAMED HORSERADISH, SRIRACHA HOT CHILI SAUCE, WORCESTERSHIRE SAUCE, AND PAPRIKA AS KEY INGREDIENTS.

INGREDIENTS

oil for deep-frying
20 fish sticks
4 large slices white bread
3½ cups arugula

RUSSIAN DRESSING

2 tablespoons mayonnaise
1 tablespoon creamed horseradish
1 tablespoon ketchup
1 tablespoon sour cream
1 tablespoon sriracha hot chili sauce
1 teaspoon Worcestershire sauce
½ teaspoon smoked paprika

1. Heat enough oil for deep-frying in a large saucepan or deep fryer to 350–375°F, or until a cube of bread browns in 30 seconds.

2. Meanwhile, mix together all of the Russian dressing ingredients in a small bowl and set aside.

3. Deep-fry the fish sticks in batches of 10 for 5 minutes or until golden, then remove with a slotted spoon, drain on paper towels, and let rest in a warm place while you cook the remaining fish sticks. Alternatively, prepare the fish sticks according to package directions.

4. Spread some of the dressing on two of the bread slices. Divide the fish sticks between two slices of bread and drizzle with the rest of the dressing. Top with the arugula and the remaining bread slices and serve immediately.

TURKEY
PAPRIKA TACOS

| SERVES: 4 | PREP TIME: 15 mins, plus marinating | COOK TIME: 8 mins |

TURKEY MAKES A REFRESHING CHANGE FROM CHICKEN IN ALMOST ANY DISH, AND ITS SOMEWHAT RICHER FLAVOR LENDS ITSELF WELL TO MEXICAN-STYLE MEALS SUCH AS THIS ONE.

INGREDIENTS

10½ ounces skinless, boneless turkey breasts, cut into strips

2 garlic cloves, crushed

2 teaspoons smoked paprika

juice of ½ lime

1 red onion, chopped

1 tomato, chopped

½ cup cooked black beans

2 cups shredded crisp lettuce

4 whole-wheat tortillas

⅓ cup shredded reduced-fat cheddar cheese

2 teaspoons hot pepper sauce

½ cup reduced-fat sour cream

1. Put the turkey strips into a shallow nonmetallic bowl. Stir in the garlic with the paprika and lime juice. Cover and let marinate for 30 minutes.

2. Meanwhile, combine the onion, tomato, beans, and lettuce in a bowl.

3. Preheat the broiler to medium-hot. Line a baking pan with foil. Put the turkey strips onto the prepared pan and cook under the preheated broiler for about 6 minutes, turning once, until golden and cooked through. Set aside.

4. Heat the tortillas under the broiler until slightly golden and crisp. Divide the turkey and the bean mixture evenly among the tortillas, arranging them on only one half of the tortilla. Sprinkle with the cheese and drizzle with the hot pepper sauce and sour cream. Fold the tacos to serve.

HOT SAUCES & RUBS

Add a spicy-hot intensity to any dish with this diverse choice of flaming sauces and rubs. The international range of sauces, from Mexican salsa to Caribbean jerk sauce, can be used as marinades or dips or can be served alongside seafood and meat dishes. From Hot-as-Hell Horseradish to Sweltering Satay and Ketchup with a Kick, there's sure to be a sauce to set you on fire.

SPICY SALSA

MAKES: about 2 cups	**PREP TIME:** 10 mins	**COOK TIME:** 20 mins

THIS SALSA PROVIDES A SPICY ACCOMPANIMENT TO ANY MEXICAN MEAL AND IS ESPECIALLY GOOD ON BURRITOS. THE FRESH TASTE OF THE CILANTRO, LIME JUICE, AND ONION SUCCESSFULLY OFFSET THE HEAT OF THE JALAPEÑOS.

INGREDIENTS

vegetable oil spray

8 plum tomatoes, halved

2–4 jalapeños, to taste, halved, cored, and seeded

4 garlic cloves

1 large onion, cut into wedges

½ cup fresh cilantro

¼ cup lime juice

1 teaspoon salt

1. Preheat the oven to 450°F and spray a baking sheet with oil.

2. Place the tomatoes, jalapeños, garlic, and onion on the prepared baking sheet and lightly spray with oil. Sprinkle with a little salt and roast in the preheated oven for 15–20 minutes, until the vegetables soften and begin to brown.

3. Put the vegetables into a food processor and pulse to a chunky paste. Add the cilantro, lime juice, and 1 teaspoon of salt and pulse until the cilantro is chopped and all of the ingredients are well combined.

4. To store, cover and refrigerate for up to one week.

RED-HOT
GARLIC & CHILI OIL

MAKES: about 1 cup	**PREP TIME:** 5 mins	**COOK TIME:** 2 hrs

CHILI OIL CAN BE USED TO SPICE UP DISHES, WHETHER DRIZZLING OVER PIZZAS OR PASTA OR ADDING A SPLASH TO MEXICAN-STYLE BEEF CHILI. THE LONGER YOU LET THE OIL SETTLE, THE HOTTER IT WILL BE.

INGREDIENTS

5 garlic cloves, halved lengthwise

2 tablespoons seeded and chopped jalapeño chile

1 teaspoon dried oregano

1 cup canola oil

1. Preheat the oven to 300°F. Combine the garlic, chile, and oregano with the oil in an ovenproof measuring cup. Put into an ovenproof dish in the center of the oven and heat for 1½–2 hours. The temperature of the oil should reach 250°F.

2. Remove from the oven, let cool, then strain through cheesecloth into a clean jar. Store in an airtight container in the refrigerator for up to one month. Alternatively, you can leave the garlic and chile pieces in the oil and strain before using.

KETCHUP
WITH A KICK

MAKES: about 2½ cups	**PREP TIME**: 15 mins	**COOK TIME**: 2 hrs 15 mins

THIS IS A GREAT RECIPE FOR THE TIME WHEN TOMATOES ARE AT THEIR CHEAPEST AND MOST PLENTIFUL. MAKE UP LARGE BATCHES OF THIS KETCHUP AND ENJOY THE TASTE OF SUMMER ALL YEAR ROUND.

INGREDIENTS

20 ripe, juicy tomatoes (about 5 pounds), coarsely chopped

2 red jalapeño chiles, coarsely chopped

1 sweet white onion, coarsely chopped

1 teaspoon salt

1 teaspoon fennel seeds

1 teaspoon black mustard seeds

1 cup apple cider vinegar or white wine vinegar

½ cup firmly packed light brown sugar

1 cinnamon stick

½ teaspoon ground nutmeg

½ teaspoon sweet paprika

1–3 teaspoons cayenne pepper

1–2 tablespoons tomato paste (optional)

pepper (optional)

1. Put the tomatoes, chiles, onion, and salt into a large saucepan over high heat. Stir until the tomatoes begin to break down, then reduce the heat to low, cover, and simmer for 30 minutes, or until the tomatoes are pulpy.

2. Meanwhile, put the fennel seeds and mustard seeds on a square of cheesecloth, bring the sides together, tie to make a bag, then set aside.

3. Pass the tomato mixture through a strainer into a large saucepan, rubbing back and forth with a wooden spoon and scraping the bottom of the strainer to produce as much paste as possible.

4. Add the spice bag and the vinegar, sugar, cinnamon stick, nutmeg, paprika, and cayenne pepper. Season with pepper, if using, then stir until the sugar dissolves. Bring to a boil, then reduce the heat and simmer, uncovered, for 1½ hours, skimming the surface as necessary, until the sauce is reduced and thickened. Transfer to a bowl and let cool.

5. Depending on how flavorful the tomatoes are, you might want to add some tomato paste. Remove the spice bag and cinnamon stick.

6. Let the ketchup cool completely. It can be used immediately, or store in an airtight container in the refrigerator for up to one month. It can also be frozen for up to three months.

HOT & FIERCE
GOCHUJANG SAUCE

MAKES: about ⅔ cup	**PREP TIME:** 5 mins	**COOK TIME:** none

KOREAN COOKS ARE USED TO MAKE ENOUGH GOCHUJANG, A FERMENTED CHILI AND SOYBEAN PASTE, IN THE SPRING TO LAST A FAMILY ALL YEAR. USE THIS SAUCE AS A MARINADE OR DIPPING SAUCE, OR FOR BASTING MEAT AND POULTRY.

INGREDIENTS

⅓ cup gochujang paste
2 teaspoon chili paste
2 tablespoons sugar
2 tablespoons hot water
2 teaspoons light soy sauce
1 teaspoon rice vinegar
1 teaspoon toasted sesame oil

1. Combine the gochujang paste, chili paste, and sugar in a heatproof bowl, then add the water, stirring to blend and dissolve the sugar and paste.

2. Stir in the soy sauce, vinegar, and sesame oil. Let the sauce cool completely.

3. The sauce can be used immediately, or store in an airtight container in the refrigerator for up to two weeks.

TIP

THIS RECIPE COMBINES AUTHENTIC FLAVOR WITH THE SPEED OF USING FERMENTED BEAN AND CHILI PASTE FROM AN ASIAN GROCERY STORE.

INTENSE TEXAN
CHILI SAUCE

MAKES: about 3 cups	**PREP TIME**: 10 mins	**COOK TIME**: 25 mins

TEXAN CHILI—OR "BIG RED" AS THE LOCALS KNOW IT—IS NOT MADE WITH BEANS, JUST MEAT, SO IT NEEDS A TASTY SAUCE LIKE THIS THAT HAS PLENTY OF HEAT AND FLAVOR.

INGREDIENTS

2 tablespoons sunflower oil or canola oil

1 red onion, chopped

2 large garlic cloves, chopped

1 green serrano chile, halved lengthwise

1 tablespoon packed dark brown sugar

2 teaspoons ground cumin

2 teaspoons dried Mexican oregano or dried thyme

2 dried morita chipotle chiles, toasted, soaked, seeded, and chopped

1 dried guajillo chile, toasted, soaked, seeded, and chopped

1 dried New Mexico red chile, toasted, soaked, seeded, and chopped

1 (14½-ounce) can diced tomatoes

½ cup beef broth or stock

½ cup strong black coffee

salt and pepper (optional)

1. Heat the oil in a saucepan over medium-high heat. Add the onion and sauté for 3–5 minutes, or until soft. Add the garlic, serrano chile, sugar, cumin, and oregano and cook for an additional minute.

2. Transfer the onion mixture to a food processor or blender. Add the chipotle chiles, guajillo chile, and New Mexico chile, tomatoes, broth or stock, and coffee and season with salt and pepper, if using. Process until pureed, scraping down the side of the processor, if necessary.

3. Transfer the puree to the pan and bring to a boil. Reduce the heat to low, cover, and simmer for 15 minutes, stirring occasionally.

4. The sauce can be used immediately, or cooled and stored in an airtight container in the refrigerator for up to three days. This sauce can be frozen for up to three months.

TEXAS-STYLE
CHILI

SERVES: 4	PREP TIME: 10 mins	COOK TIME: 3 hrs

TEXANS DON'T TOLERATE BEANS OR ANY OTHER ADDITIONS IN THEIR BIG BOWLS OF CHILI. WHAT YOU SEE IS WHAT YOU GET—JUST CHUNKS OF BEEF AND HOT CHILI SAUCE. IT'S PLAIN AND SIMPLE, AND UTTERLY DELICIOUS.

INGREDIENTS

2 tablespoons rendered bacon fat, sunflower oil, or canola oil, plus extra, if needed

1½ pounds beef chuck steak, cut into 1-inch cubes

1 large onion, finely chopped

1 large garlic clove, finely chopped

1 tablespoon crushed red pepper flakes

3 cups Intense Texan Chili Sauce (see previous page)

1 tablespoon masa harina

1 tablespoon red wine vinegar

salt and pepper (optional)

cooked rice and sour cream, to serve

1. Heat the fat in a large, heavy saucepan over medium heat. Season the beef with salt and pepper, if using. Working in batches, add the beef to the pan and cook, stirring occasionally, until brown on all sides, adding extra fat, if needed. Set aside the beef and juices.

2. Pour off all but 1 tablespoon of the fat. Add the onion to the pan and cook for 3–5 minutes, or until soft. Add the garlic and red pepper flakes and cook for an additional minute. Return the beef and all the juices to the pan and stir in the Texan Sauce. Cover and bring to a boil, then reduce the heat to low and simmer for 2¼–2½ hours, until the beef is tender.

3. Put the harina into a small bowl and stir in the vinegar. Stir the mixture into the chili and simmer for 10 minutes, or until the chili thickens. Season with salt and pepper. Serve in bowls over rice, with sour cream.

CHIMICHURRI
SWELTERING SAUCE

| **MAKES**: about ¾ cup | **PREP TIME**: 5 mins, plus marinating | **COOK TIME**: none |

NO LATIN AMERICAN BARBECUE IS COMPLETE WITHOUT A BOWL OF ZINGY, FRESH
CHIMICHURRI; A BLEND OF HERBS AND CHILES. THIS HOT-AND-SPICY VERSION HAS A
THAI CHILE TO CRANK UP THE HEAT. SERVE WITH ALL GRILLED AND ROASTED MEATS OR
A SELECTION OF VEGETABLE STICKS.

INGREDIENTS

¾ cup fresh cilantro leaves

⅔ cup fresh flat-leaf parsley leaves

4 garlic cloves,
coarsely chopped

1–2 green Thai chiles, finely chopped

1 teaspoon crushed red pepper flakes

1 teaspoon dried Mexican oregano or
1 teaspoon dried thyme (optional)

½ cup sunflower oil or canola oil

¼ cup red wine vinegar or white
wine vinegar

salt and pepper

1. Put the cilantro, parsley, garlic, chiles, red pepper flakes, oregano, if using, and salt and pepper into a food processor and finely chop, scraping down the sides, if necessary. Do not blend to a paste.

2. With the motor running, slowly drizzle in the oil. Add the vinegar and adjust the seasoning if necessary.

3. The sauce can be used immediately, but is best if you store it in an airtight container in the refrigerator for at least 3 hours to let the flavors blend. The sauce will keep for up to three days in the refrigerator if covered with an extra layer of oil, although its bright-green color will dull. Pour off the oil before serving.

TIP
IF YOU DON'T WANT TO
USE A FOOD PROCESSOR,
FINELY CHOP THE CILANTRO,
PARSLEY, AND GARLIC,
THEN MIX TOGETHER IN A
NONMETALLIC BOWL.

JAMAICAN JERK
SAUCE

MAKES: about 1¼ cups	**PREP TIME**: 10 mins, plus marinating	**COOK TIME**: none

THIS HOT, HOT, HOT CARIBBEAN FAVORITE CAN BE USED AS A MARINADE OR AS A BASTING SAUCE WHILE BARBECUING. CHICKEN IS ITS TRADITIONAL PARTNER, BUT IT ALSO ADDS A SUNNY CARIBBEAN TASTE TO MOST MEAT AND SEAFOOD DISHES.

INGREDIENTS

¼ cup freshly squeezed lemon juice

¼ cup dark soy sauce

¼ cup sunflower oil

¼ cup red wine vinegar or white wine vinegar

4 red Scotch bonnet chiles or habanero chiles, seeded and finely chopped

4 scallions, finely chopped

1 shallot, finely chopped

1-inch piece fresh ginger, grated

2 tablespoons packed light brown sugar

2 teaspoons dried thyme

1 teaspoon ground allspice

½ teaspoon ground cinnamon

¼ teaspoon ground cloves

salt and pepper

1. Mix together the lemon juice, soy sauce, oil, and vinegar in a large nonmetallic bowl.

2. Stir in the remaining ingredients and season with salt and pepper, stirring until the sugar dissolves. Set aside for at least 30 minutes for the flavors to blend.

3. The sauce can be used immediately, or store in an airtight container in the refrigerator for up to one month.

JERK CHICKEN

SERVES: 4	PREP TIME: 10 mins, plus marinating	COOK TIME: 40 mins

AUTHENTIC JAMAICAN JERK CHICKEN HAS A UNIQUE FLAVOR FROM BEING SLOWLY COOKED OVER PIMENTO, OR ALLSPICE, WOOD. WHILE THE FLAVOR HERE ISN'T EXACTLY THE SAME, IT DOES GIVES YOU THE JAMAICAN JERK HEAT.

INGREDIENTS

4 chicken legs

1¼ cups Jamaican Jerk Sauce (see previous page)

sunflower oil, for brushing

coleslaw, pineapple, and rice salad, to serve (optional)

1. Use a fork to pierce the chicken legs all over. Put the chicken into a bowl in a single layer. Pour the Jamaican Jerk Sauce over the poultry and rub in. Cover the bowl with plastic wrap and marinate in the refrigerator for at least 4 hours, or for up to 36 hours.

2. Remove the chicken from the refrigerator 30 minutes in advance of cooking. Light a barbecue and heat until the coals turn gray. Alternatively, preheat the broiler to high and oil the broiler rack.

3. Place the chicken pieces on the rack, fleshy side down. Brush with some of the sauce remaining in the bowl and cook for 20 minutes.

4. Turn the chicken over and cook for an additional 20 minutes, brushing with the remaining sauce, or until it is cooked all the way through and the juices run clear when the thickest part of the flesh is pierced with a sharp knife.

5. Transfer the chicken to a warm plate and let rest for 5 minutes. Use a cleaver to cut each leg into four pieces, then serve with coleslaw, pineapple, and rice salad, if using.

LOUISIANA
HOT PEPPER SAUCE

MAKES: about ½ cup	**PREP TIME:** 5 mins	**COOK TIME:** 15 mins

THIS SAUCE IS TRADITIONALLY MADE WITH FRESH, SMALL TABASCO CHILES, BUT THEY CAN BE DIFFICULT TO FIND, SO DRIED CAYENNE OR THAI CHILES ARE USED IN THIS RECIPE TO GIVE THE SAME TONGUE-TINGLING SENSATION.

INGREDIENTS

2 ounces dried red cayenne peppers or dried red thai chiles, stems removed, coarsely chopped, and soaked for 30 minutes

½ cup white wine vinegar

½ teaspoon salt

1. Turn the exhaust fan to high or open a window. Drain the soaked chiles. Put the chiles, vinegar, and salt into a small saucepan. Cover the pan and bring to a boil, then reduce the heat to low and simmer for 10–12 minutes, or until soft.

2. Tip the contents of the pan into a small food processor or blender and puree, scraping down the side of the processor if necessary. Strain the blended mixture to remove the seeds. Transfer the sauce to a nonmetallic bowl and let cool completely.

3. Let the sauce mature for at least 2 weeks in an airtight container in the refrigerator before using. The sauce will then keep in the refrigerator for an additional month.

PIQUANT PICO DE GALLO SAUCE

MAKES: about ¾ cup	**PREP TIME**: 10 mins, plus resting	**COOK TIME**: none

HOT AND FRESH FLAVORS MINGLE IN THIS SIMPLE MEXICAN SALSA-LIKE SAUCE, WHICH ADDS A BURST OF CHILE HEAT TO EVERYTHING FROM A BOWL OF TORTILLA CHIPS TO GRILLED MEAT AND TACOS.

INGREDIENTS

⅔ cup tomato puree or tomato sauce

2 tablespoons freshly squeezed lime juice or orange juice, or to taste

2 large pickled garlic cloves or fresh garlic cloves, minced

½ sweet white onion, finely chopped

2 tablespoons pickled jalapeño chiles, drained and finely chopped

½ teaspoon ancho chili powder

salt and pepper (optional)

small handful of cilantro leaves, finely chopped, to garnish

1. Combine the tomato puree or sauce and lime juice in a nonmetallic bowl and season with salt and pepper, if using. Add all the remaining ingredients, except the cilantro leaves.

2. The sauce can be served immediately, but it will benefit from resting at room temperature for 30 minutes for the flavors to blend. Stir well before serving and adjust the lime juice and salt and pepper, if using. Sprinkle with cilantro just before serving.

3. If there is any leftover sauce, pour a layer of olive oil over it, cover, and store in the refrigerator for up to three days. Stir in the oil just before serving and garnish with chopped fresh cilantro.

TIP

STILL NOT HOT ENOUGH? THEN USE RED OR GREEN THAI CHILES INSTEAD OF THE JALAPEÑOS.

INGREDIENTS FOR HOT SAUCES

With a little judicious selection, common pantry ingredients can produce an astonishing variety of flavors in your sauces. Use the ingredients below and experiment to suit your taste.

Chiles are the essential ingredient in most hot sauce recipes, and they come in a wide range of varieties and heats.

Harissa paste is a strong and aromatic dark-red paste (see opposite, above left) made from chiles, spices, and herbs, used for adding heat and flavor to North African food. The base ingredients are chiles, garlic, oil, ground cumin, coriander, and caraway seeds.

Herbs and spices provide a depth of flavor, whether they are fresh or dried. Jamaican Jerk Sauce, for example, wouldn't taste authentic without dried allspice, and Chimichurri Sweltering Sauce relies on a medley of fresh herbs.

Horseradish is a thick, white root that, when freshly grated, has an intense, sharp, hot flavor. Mixing grated horseradish with lemon juice helps prolong the sharpness. If buying grated horseradish, avoid horseradish sauce, which is mixed with cream, or grated horseradish in vinegar.

Mustard is one of the most popular and widely used spices and condiments and will add a hot punch to a meal. The level of heat is defined by the seed type and preparation. Choose bright-yellow dry mustard for the hottest flavor.

Paprika is the finely ground powder of dried sweet red bell peppers—its heat ranges from mild and sweet to intensely hot. It needs to be fresh: otherwise the flavor is lost.

Oil is essential for cooking chiles and other ingredients and for adding body to sauces. Keep a selection, such as sunflower, canola, peanut, and olive, to have a variety of flavor options on hand.

Salt is used to bring out individual flavors.

Sambal oelek paste is a red sauce (see opposite, below right) from Indonesia. It is made with chiles, salt, and citrus juice or vinegar; comes in varying degrees of hotness; and is sold in supermarkets and specialty food stores.

Sichuan peppercorns have an unmistakable flavor—the heat blends with a lingering tingling sensation on your tongue and cheeks (see opposite, bottom left).

Sugars, both white and brown, will provide a counterpoint to hot spiciness and act as a preservative. Always dissolve sugar before bringing a sauce to a boil to prevent crystals from forming.

Vinegar provides a sour background, as well as acts as a preservative. Traditional American sauces often contain distilled white vinegar, but apple cider vinegars, red wine vinegar, and white wine vinegar are also good.

Wasabi, also known as Japanese horseradish (see opposite, above right), comes from a root and packs a real punch. It is pungent and hot, and it is sold as a stem for grating, as well as already prepared as a paste or in powder form.

PERI-PERI
AT YOUR PERIL SAUCE

MAKES: about ⅓ cup	PREP TIME: 10 mins	COOK TIME: 10 mins

THIS PERI-PERI SAUCE IS AS GOOD AS ANY YOU WOULD FIND AT WELL-KNOWN RESTAURANTS. YOU CAN PAIR IT WITH FRIED CHICKEN WINGS TO CREATE A DELICIOUS HOT-AND-SPICY MEAL.

INGREDIENTS

¼ cup sunflower oil

24 peri-peri chiles or Thai chiles, chopped

½ onion, finely chopped

4 large garlic cloves, chopped

1 teaspoon sweet paprika

¼ teaspoon ground allspice

⅓ cup freshly squeezed lemon juice, or to taste

2 tablespoons water

finely grated zest of 1 lemon

salt and pepper (optional)

1. Turn the exhaust fan to high or open a window to let air circulate. Heat the oil in a saucepan over medium heat. Add the chiles and onion and cook for 3 minutes. Add the garlic, paprika, and allspice and stir for an additional minute.

2. Add ¼ cup of the lemon juice and the water and season with salt and pepper, if using. Bring to a boil, stirring. Reduce the heat to low, cover, and simmer for 5 minutes, or until the chiles are soft. Uncover and check once or twice to make sure the garlic doesn't burn.

3. If you would like a smooth, restaurant-style sauce, transfer the ingredients to a small food processor or blender and puree, or leave as a chunky sauce, if preferred. Stir in the remaining lemon juice. Adjust the seasoning and lemon juice, if desired. Stir in the lemon zest.

4. The sauce can be used immediately, or let it cool completely and store in an airtight container in the refrigerator for up to two weeks.

SPICY ROASTED TOMATO SAUCE

MAKES: about ¾ cup	PREP TIME: 10 mins	COOK TIME: 45 mins

THIS SAUCE, WITH ITS PAPRIKA AND SHERRY INGREDIENTS, HAS A SPANISH FLAVOR AND IS GREAT WHEN SERVED AS A DIP WITH TORTILLA CHIPS OR AS AN ACCOMPANIMENT TO A SPANISH OMELET AND FRENCH FRIES.

INGREDIENTS

6 vine-ripened tomatoes

1 red bell pepper, cut into quarters and seeded

1 garlic clove, unpeeled

1 red onion, cut into quarters

¼ cup olive oil

1 small red jalapeño chile, minced

1 teaspoon hot paprika

1 tablespoon sherry

salt and pepper

1. Preheat the oven to 350°F.

2. Lay out the vegetables on a large baking pan, brush with olive oil, then roast in the oven, turning once halfway through cooking, for about 45 minutes or until they are blistered and slightly charred.

3. Let cool. When cool enough to handle, peel the tomatoes and red bell pepper, and squeeze the garlic from its skin. Transfer the tomato, red bell pepper, garlic flesh, and onion to a food processor and process to a fairly smooth consistency.

4. Spoon the mixture into a large serving bowl and stir in the chile, paprika, and sherry. Season with salt and pepper. The sauce can be used immediately or let it cool completely and store in an airtight container in the refrigerator for up to one week.

TIP

THE TABLESPOON OF SHERRY IN THIS RECIPE CAN ALSO BE REPLACED BY MADEIRA, WHICH IS A FORTIFIED WINE FROM PORTUGAL.

HABANERO
CHILI RUB

MAKES: about ⅔ cup	PREP TIME: 10 mins, plus chilling	COOK TIME: none

THE HABANERO CHILE IS ONE OF THE HOTTEST CHILES IN THE WORLD, RATED 100,000–350,000 ON THE SCOVILLE SCALE. SO IF YOU'RE CHOOSING TO USE THIS RUB, BE PREPARED FOR YOUR TASTE BUDS TO TINGLE.

INGREDIENTS

2 tablespoons paprika

1–2 tablespoons dried crushed habanero chiles or chili powder

1 tablespoon garlic powder

1 tablespoon onion powder

1 tablespoon ground cumin

1 tablespoon salt

2 teaspoons pepper

2 teaspoons packed light brown sugar

1 teaspoon cayenne pepper

½ teaspoon freshly grated nutmeg

1. Mix all the ingredients together in a small bowl until thoroughly combined.

2. Rub the mixture thoroughly into meat, poultry, fish, or seafood 1–2 hours before cooking.

3. Put in a shallow dish, cover tightly, and chill in the refrigerator until required.

HOT-AS-HELL
HORSERADISH SAUCE

MAKES: about ⅔ cup	**PREP TIME**: 10 mins	**COOK TIME**: none

THIS EASY SAUCE GETS ITS PUNCHY HEAT FROM FRESHLY GRATED HORSERADISH. IT'S TRADITIONALLY ADDED TO SEAFOOD COCKTAILS, BUT YOU CAN ADD A SPOONFUL OR TWO TO HOMEMADE TOMATO SOUP FOR AN EXTRA KICK.

INGREDIENTS

½ cup ketchup, plus extra, if needed

1-inch piece horseradish, finely grated, or 1 tablespoon grated horseradish

1 tablespoon freshly squeezed lemon juice, or to taste, plus extra if needed

pepper (optional)

1. Put the ketchup and horseradish into a bowl and stir to combine.

2. Add the lemon juice and pepper, if using. Stir to combine, then add extra lemon juice if desired.

3. The sauce can be served immediately, or stored in an airtight container in the refrigerator for up to three weeks. After one or two days, the sauce will thicken, so you will need to beat in extra ketchup or lemon juice with a fork when ready to serve.

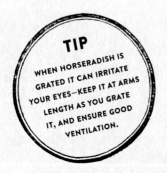

TIP
WHEN HORSERADISH IS GRATED IT CAN IRRITATE YOUR EYES—KEEP IT AT ARMS LENGTH AS YOU GRATE IT, AND ENSURE GOOD VENTILATION.

RAS EL HANOUT
CARIBBEAN RUB

| MAKES: about ½ cup | PREP TIME: 10 mins, plus chilling | COOK TIME: none |

COMBINED WITH OIL, THIS HOT CARIBBEAN FAVORITE CAN BE USED AS A MARINADE OR AS A BASTING SAUCE WHILE BARBECUING. CHICKEN IS ITS TRADITIONAL PARTNER, BUT IT ADDS A CARIBBEAN TASTE TO MEAT AND SEAFOOD DISHES.

INGREDIENTS

2 teaspoons ground cumin
2 teaspoons ground ginger
2 teaspoons ground turmeric
2 teaspoons ground cinnamon
2 teaspoons ground cardamom seeds
2 teaspoons ground coriander seeds
2 teaspoons ground ginger
2 teaspoons ground allspice
2 teaspoons saffron threads
1 teaspoon freshly grated nutmeg
1 teaspoon salt
1 teaspoon pepper
½ teaspoon ground cloves

1. Mix all the ingredients together in a small bowl until they are thoroughly combined.

2. Rub the mixture thoroughly into meat, poultry, fish, or seafood just before cooking.

3. Put in a shallow dish, cover tightly, and chill in the refrigerator until required.

RAS EL HANOUT
GARLIC & THYME
ROAST LEG OF LAMB

| SERVES: 6–8 | PREP TIME: 15 mins | COOK TIME: 3 hrs 30 mins, plus resting |

ROASTING THIS SPICED LEG OF LAMB SLOWLY WILL GIVE YOU MELTINGLY TENDER MEAT AND WILL FILL YOUR KITCHEN WITH WONDERFUL AROMAS.

INGREDIENTS

20 fresh lemon thyme sprigs

8 garlic cloves, peeled

4 teaspoons sea salt flakes

¼ cup ras el hanout
(see previous page)

¼ cup olive oil

1 (4½–5½-pound) leg of lamb

2 heads of garlic, halved horizontally

2 onions, cut into quarters

1¼ cups water

salt and pepper, to serve

1 tablespoon Greek-style plain yogurt,
to serve

1. Preheat the oven to 300°F. Strip the leaves from half the lemon thyme and put them into a mortar and pestle. Add the garlic cloves and 3 teaspoons of the salt and crush. Add the ras el hanout and oil, and mix to form a coarse paste.

2. Put the lamb into a roasting pan. Using a sharp knife, make several small slits in the skin. Rub in the spice paste, working it into the slits well. Sprinkle with the remaining salt, put the halved heads of garlic and quartered onions alongside it, sprinkle with the remaining lemon thyme, then pour the water around it.

3. Roast for 30 minutes, uncovered. Baste the lamb with the cooking liquid and cover the pan with aluminum foil. Roast for an additional 3 hours, basting every half an hour.

4. Transfer the lamb to a serving plate, add the onions and garlic, and let rest, covered in foil, for 30 minutes.

5. For the gravy, skim the excess oil off the liquid and season with a pinch of salt and pepper. Stir the yogurt into the gravy and serve alongside the roast lamb and onions.

RED-HOT
GREEN SAUCE

MAKES: about 1¾ cups	**PREP TIME**: 10 mins	**COOK TIME**: none

THIS COMBINATION OF PICKLED JALAPEÑOS AND SMOKED HOT PAPRIKA IS PACKED FULL OF PUNCH, MAKING STORE-BOUGHT SALSA SEEM MILD AND UNEXCEPTIONAL! THE SAUCE IS ZESTY AND HOT, AND THE FRESH GREEN COLOR LOOKS APPETIZING IN A CONTRASTING BOWL.

INGREDIENTS

14 drained canned tomatillos (about 16 ounces), stem ends removed, and coarsely chopped

4 scallions, chopped

2 large garlic cloves, coarsely chopped

2 tablespoons drained pickled jalapeño chiles, chopped

handful of cilantro leaves

freshly squeezed lime juice (optional)

1 teaspoon honey

½ teaspoon smoked hot paprika

salt and pepper (optional)

1 tablespoon finely chopped fresh cilantro, to garnish

1. Put the tomatillos, scallions, garlic, chiles, and cilantro leaves into a food processor and process in short blasts to finely chop, but not puree.

2. Transfer the mixture to a bowl. Season with salt and pepper, if using, then add the lime juice, if using, and the honey. Stir in the paprika.

3. The sauce can be used immediately, or stored in an airtight container in the refrigerator for up to four days, although the color will start to dull after three days. Sprinkle with the chopped cilantro just before serving.

SWELTERING
SATAY SAUCE

| SERVES: about ¾ cup | PREP TIME: 10 mins | COOK TIME: 5 mins |

THE TRADITIONALLY MILD PEANUT SAUCE IS HEATED UP IN THIS VERSION WITH THE ADDITION OF AN INDONESIAN CHILI PASTE CALLED SAMBAL OELEK. IT IS SOLD IN MOST ASIAN FOOD STORES BUT THE INTENSITY OF THE HEAT VARIES WITH THE BRAND.

INGREDIENTS

2 tablespoons sunflower oil

2 shallots, finely chopped

1 large garlic clove, finely chopped

1-inch piece fresh ginger, finely chopped

1–3 teaspoons Indonesian chili paste (sambal oelek)

1 cup coconut milk

⅓ cup chunky peanut butter

1 teaspoon tamarind paste or freshly squeezed lime juice, or to taste

1 teaspoon dark soy sauce, or to taste

¼ cup water, if needed

4 red jalapeño chiles, seeded and thinly sliced

salt and pepper (optional)

1. Heat the oil in a wok over high heat until hot. Add the shallots, garlic, and ginger and stir-fry for 1–2 minutes, or until the shallots are soft and just beginning to brown. Stir in the chili paste and continue cooking for an additional 30 seconds.

2. Add the coconut milk and peanut butter, stirring until blended. Stir in the tamarind paste and soy sauce, season with pepper, if using, and continue stirring over medium heat for 2–3 minutes. If the mixture looks separated, stir in the water and beat well. Stir in the chiles. Adjust the seasoning, if necessary, and add extra chili paste, tamarind paste, and soy sauce, if desired.

3. The sauce can be served hot or at room temperature, or let it cool completely and store in an airtight container in the refrigerator for up to one week.

NACHO SAUCE

| **MAKES**: about 1¼ cups | **PREP TIME**: 5 mins | **COOK TIME**: 15 mins |

THIS CREAMY NACHO SAUCE GETS ITS HEAT FROM DRY MUSTARD, HOT SAUCE, AND FINELY CHOPPED CHILES. YOU CAN TOP TORTILLA CHIPS WITH THE SAUCE OR ALTERNATIVELY MIX IT WITH COOKED PASTA OR ADD IT TO BAKED POTATOES.

INGREDIENTS

1 cup shredded sharp cheddar cheese

3 tablespoons cornstarch

1 tablespoon dry mustard

1 cup milk

2 tablespoons cream cheese

2 teaspoon sriracha or other hot chili sauce

2 red or green jalapeño chiles, finely chopped

salt and pepper (optional)

1. Mix together the cheddar cheese, cornstarch, and dry mustard in a heatproof bowl, then set aside.

2. Put the milk into a saucepan and bring just to a boil. Stir ¼ cup of the hot milk into the cheese mixture, stirring until well blended. Add the cheese mixture to the milk, whisking vigorously.

3. Bring the mixture back just to a boil, then reduce the heat and simmer, whisking frequently, for 5 minutes, until the sauce is smooth and has reduced. Remove the pan from the heat and stir in the cream cheese and chili sauce. Season with salt and pepper, if using, then stir in the chiles.

4. The sauce can be used immediately, or let it cool completely and stored in an airtight container in the refrigerator for up to three days. To serve, reheat gently without boiling.

TIP

DO NOT ADD THE CORNSTARCH OR DRY MUSTARD DIRECTLY TO THE HOT MILK OR LUMPS WILL FORM. WHISK TO BE SURE OF A SMOOTH MIXTURE.

DANGEROUS
ADOBO SAUCE

MAKES: about 1¼ cups	**PREP TIME**: 10 mins	**COOK TIME**: 1½–1¾ hrs

CHIPOTLE CHILES ARE DRIED JALAPEÑO CHILES, WHICH ARE AVAILABLE IN TWO FORMS, MORITA OR MECO. MECO CHIPOTLES GIVE A SMOKIER FLAVOR THAT WORKS WELL WITH SLOW-COOKED MEAT DISHES.

INGREDIENTS

¼ cup tomato paste

2½ cups water

⅓ cup white wine vinegar

12 dried chipotle chiles, stems removed

4 garlic cloves, crushed

½ red onion, minced

2 tablespoons packed light brown sugar

1 tablespoon ground cumin

1 tablespoon dried Mexican oregano or dried thyme

2 teaspoons hot smoked paprika

2 teaspoons cayenne pepper

½ teaspoon salt

pepper (optional)

1. Dissolve the tomato paste in the water and vinegar in a deep saucepan. Stir in the other ingredients and season with pepper, if using. Cover and bring to a boil.

2. Uncover, reduce the heat to low, and simmer for 1¼–1½ hours, or until the chiles are soft and the sauce thickens.

3. Transfer the sauce to a blender or food processor and puree. Strain the sauce through a strainer into a bowl, rubbing back and forth with a wooden spoon and scraping the bottom of the strainer to produce as much sauce as possible. Set aside to cool completely.

4. The sauce can be used immediately, or store in an airtight container in the refrigerator for up to three weeks.

MEATBALLS IN
ADOBO SAUCE

SERVES: 4	PREP TIME: 20 mins	COOK TIME: 30–35 mins

WHEN YOU'RE EXPECTING CHILE LOVERS FOR DINNER, THIS IS A WONDERFUL QUICK-AND-EASY DISH TO SERVE. THE SAUCE IS SPICY HOT AND ANY LEFTOVERS WILL MAKE A GREAT TACO FILLING.

INGREDIENTS

⅓ cup dried bread crumbs

3–4 tablespoons milk

3 tablespoons all-purpose flour, for dusting

8 ounces ground round beef

8 ounces lean ground pork

4 large garlic cloves, finely chopped

2 eggs, beaten

3 tablespoons finely chopped fresh parsley or cilantro

1 teaspoon ground cinnamon

1 teaspoon sweet paprika

¼ cup sunflower oil, for frying, plus extra if needed

1¼ cups Dangerous Adobo Sauce (see previous page)

1 cup coarsely chopped mozzarella cheese

¼ cup shredded cheddar cheese

salt and pepper (optional)

1. Combine the bread crumbs and milk in a bowl and let soak for 10 minutes. Put the flour on a plate and set aside. Preheat the oven to 400°F.

2. Combine the beef, pork, garlic, eggs, parsley, cinnamon, and paprika with the bread crumb mixture in a large bowl. Season with salt and pepper, if using, and stir to combine.

3. Using wet hands, shape the mixture into 24 equal balls. Heat the oil in a large skillet over medium heat. Working in batches, lightly roll the meatballs in the flour, shaking off the excess. Add the meatballs to the pan and cook, turning, until brown all over, then transfer to a baking dish.

4. Pour the Adobo Sauce over the meatballs in the dish, then sprinkle with the mozzarella cheese and cheddar cheese. Bake in the preheated oven for 15–20 minutes, or until the meatballs are cooked through, the sauce is hot, and the cheese is melting.

5. Meanwhile, preheat the broiler to high. Place the dish under the broiler and brown for 2–3 minutes.

VEGETABLE MAINS & SIDES

This chapter focuses on vegetable dishes—be prepared, because they are charged with smoky spices and hot chiles. Eggplant, zucchini, butternut squash, and celeriac are all given the treatment. Our selection ranges from Celeriac, Fennel & Peach Slaw and Gratin of Green Chiles to Sweet Potato & Broccoli Burgers and Smoky Barbecue Beans.

EGGPLANT
STUFFED WITH BULGUR WHEAT

SERVES: 4	PREP TIME: 35 mins	COOK TIME: 55 mins

A GOOD SOURCE OF VITAMINS, MINERALS, AND FIBER, PURPLE EGGPLANTS WORK WELL WITH SPICES IN THIS WHOLESOME DISH. FIBER-RICH BULGUR WHEAT PROVIDES THE BASE FOR THE HERBY-VEGETABLE STUFFING.

INGREDIENTS

1 teaspoon ground cumin

1 teaspoon ground coriander

1 teaspoon paprika

1 teaspoon crushed red pepper flakes

2 tablespoons olive oil

2 eggplant, cut in half lengthwise

1 red onion, coarsely chopped

2 garlic cloves, chopped

1 cup fine bulgur wheat

1 cup vegetable broth or stock

3 tablespoons coarsely chopped fresh cilantro

3 tablespoons coarsely chopped fresh mint

1 cup crumbled feta cheese

⅓ cup slivered almonds, toasted

1½ tablespoons lemon juice

2 teaspoons pomegranate molasses

salt and pepper (optional)

1 tablespoon chopped fresh mint, to garnish

1 teaspoon pomegranate molasses, to garnish

½ cup Greek-style plain yogurt, to garnish

¼ cup pomegranate seeds, to garnish

1. Preheat the oven to 350°F. Mix the cumin, ground coriander, paprika, crushed red pepper flakes, and 1½ tablespoons of olive oil in a small bowl. Use a sharp knife to slice the eggplant flesh in a diagonal, crisscross pattern, without piercing the skin. Drizzle the cumin mixture over the eggplant, allowing it to sink into the cuts. Place the eggplant halves on a baking sheet and roast in the oven for 35 minutes.

2. Meanwhile, heat the remaining 1½ teaspoons of olive oil in a large skillet over medium heat. Add the onion and garlic and sauté for 3–4 minutes, or until softened. Reduce the heat, add the bulgur wheat, and stir well. Reduce the heat to low, pour in the vegetable broth or stock, and stir until the liquid has been absorbed. Remove the mixture from the pan and transfer to a large bowl.

3. Remove the eggplant from the oven and let rest for 10 minutes. Keep the oven on. Using a tablespoon, scoop out the center of the eggplant, leaving a clear edge to support the filling.

4. Add the eggplant flesh to the bulgur mixture. Stir in the fresh cilantro, mint, feta, almonds, lemon juice, and pomegranate molasses. Stir well and season with salt and pepper, if using.

5. Divide the stuffing among the eggplant halves and return to the oven for 15 minutes. Serve immediately, garnished with the fresh mint, molasses, yogurt, and pomegranate seeds.

SPICED VEGETABLE & HALLOUMI SKEWERS

SERVES: 8	PREP TIME: 25 mins	COOK TIME: 30 minutes

THESE SPICED SKEWERS MAKE A GREAT VEGETARIAN OPTION FOR BARBECUES AND, SIMPLE TO MAKE, THEY ARE PERFECT FOR A CROWD. YOU WILL NEED 16 WOODEN SKEWERS FOR THIS RECIPE.

INGREDIENTS

8 ounces cremini mushrooms, halved or quartered depending on size

8 ounces halloumi or queso paisa cheese, cut into ⅝-inch chunks

1 large eggplant, cut into ¾-inch chunks

3 cups cherry tomatoes

1 tablespoon ras el hanout

1 teaspoon sea salt flakes

3 tablespoons olive oil

pinch of sea salt flakes

1. Preheat the oven to 350°F. Soak 16 wooden skewers in water for 20 minutes, then drain well.

2. Put the mushrooms, cheese, eggplant, and cherry tomatoes in a large bowl and toss well. Add the ras el hanout, 1 teaspoon of salt, and the oil and toss again.

3. Thread the vegetables and cheese onto the skewers in any combination, then place them on two large baking pans. Roast for 30 minutes, or until the vegetables are tender. Sprinkle with a large pinch of salt and serve two skewers per person.

TIP

IF YOU WANT, ASSEMBLE THE SKEWERS IN ADVANCE AND LET THEM MARINATE FOR A FEW HOURS IN THE REFRIGERATOR BEFORE COOKING.

RED KIDNEY BEAN STEW

SERVES: 4	PREP TIME: 20 mins	COOK TIME: 30–35 mins

HIGH IN FIBER, THIS DELICIOUS NORTHERN INDIAN DISH OF SPICED RED KIDNEY BEANS IS BEST SERVED WITH RICE AND WARM FLATBREADS. IT CAN EASILY BE MADE A DAY AHEAD—SIMPLY REHEAT IT AND SERVE WITH THE YOGURT.

INGREDIENTS

2 tablespoons vegetable oil or peanut oil

2 teaspoons cumin seeds

2 onions, finely chopped

2 teaspoons grated fresh ginger

6 garlic cloves, crushed

2 fresh green chiles, finely chopped

2 large tomatoes, coarsely chopped

2 teaspoons ground coriander

1 teaspoon ground cumin

¼ teaspoon ground turmeric

1 teaspoon garam masala

1 (29-ounce) can red kidney beans, drained and rinsed

1 teaspoon palm sugar or brown sugar

2 cups warm water

1 teaspoon salt

¼ cup finely chopped fresh cilantro, to garnish

2 tablespoons plain yogurt, to serve

1. Heat the oil in a large saucepan and add the cumin seeds. When they stop crackling, add the onions and sauté until soft.

2. Add the ginger and garlic and sauté for 2 minutes. Add the chiles, tomatoes, ground coriander, cumin, turmeric, and garam masala and stir-fry for 12–15 minutes.

3. Add the red kidney beans, sugar, water, and salt and cook for 10–12 minutes, or until the beans are soft.

4. Remove from the heat and transfer to a serving dish. Garnish with the chopped cilantro and serve with the yogurt.

TIP
CANNED BEANS ARE USED IN THIS RECIPE FOR SPEED. IF USING DRIED BEANS, COOK ACCORDING TO THE PACKAGE DIRECTIONS BEFORE USING.

BENGALI
VEGETABLE STEW

SERVES: 4	PREP TIME: 30 mins, plus standing	COOK TIME: 30–35 mins

THIS TRADITIONAL BENGALI VEGETABLE STEW USES A MIXTURE OF CHOPPED VEGETABLES AND IS COOKED WITH A MUSTARD SEED AND WHITE POPPY SEED PASTE. PANCH PHORAN IS A BENGALI SPICE MIXTURE MADE OF FENUGREEK SEEDS, FENNEL SEEDS, MUSTARD SEEDS, NIGELLA SEEDS, AND CUMIN SEEDS.

INGREDIENTS

⅓ cup plus 2 teaspoons white poppy seeds (khus khus)

3 tablespoons black mustard seeds

2 teaspoons grated fresh ginger

¼ cup vegetable oil or peanut oil

2 fresh green chiles, halved lengthwise

1 tablespoon panch phoran

2 small fresh bitter melons (kerala), cut into ⅝-inch cubes

2 potatoes, peeled and cut into ⅝-inch cubes

1 eggplant, cut into ⅝-inch cubes

1 zucchini, cut into ⅝-inch cubes

1 carrot, cut into ⅝-inch cubes

1 tomato, finely chopped

⅔ cup fresh or frozen peas

1¾ cups cold water

¼ teaspoon ground turmeric

2 teaspoons salt

1 teaspoon palm sugar or brown sugar

½ cup milk

1. Soak the white poppy seeds and 2 tablespoons of the mustard seeds in warm water for 1 hour. Drain and blend with the ginger to make a paste.

2. Heat the oil in a large skillet and add the remaining mustard seeds and the chiles. When the mustard seeds start to pop, add the panch phoran and all the vegetables. Add half the water and stir to mix well, then cover tightly and cook, stirring frequently, over medium heat for 10–12 minutes.

3. Add half the white poppy seed-and-mustard seed paste, the turmeric, and salt. Add the remaining water and cook, stirring frequently, over low-medium heat for an additional 10–15 minutes.

4. Add the remaining white poppy seed-and-mustard seed paste, the sugar, and milk and cook for an additional 5 minutes, or until the vegetables are tender. Serve hot.

SPICY COUSCOUS WITH NUTS, DATES & APRICOTS

SERVES: 4	PREP TIME: 15 mins	COOK TIME: 15 mins

COUSCOUS COMBINED WITH DRIED FRUIT AND NUTS IS DELICIOUS SERVED WITH GRILLED MEATS AND SPICY STEWS. TRADITIONALLY, A FRUITY COUSCOUS WOULD ALSO BE DUSTED WITH CINNAMON AND SERVED ON ITS OWN, OFTEN AS A PALATE CLEANSER.

INGREDIENTS

2 cups couscous
1¼ cups boiling water
½ teaspoon sea salt flakes
2 tablespoons olive oil
1–2 tablespoons clarified butter
large pinch of saffron threads
1 cup blanched almonds
1 cup unsalted pistachio nuts
1–2 teaspoons ras el hanout
¾ cup thinly sliced dates
¾ cup thinly sliced dried apricots
2 teaspoons ground cinnamon, to garnish

1. Put the couscous into a shallow heatproof bowl. Put the boiling water into a heatproof bowl, stir in the salt, then pour it over the couscous, cover, and let stand for 10 minutes.

2. Drizzle the oil over the couscous. Using your fingers, rub it into the grains to break up the lumps.

3. Heat the butter in a heavy skillet over medium heat. Add the saffron, almonds, and pistachio nuts and cook for 1–2 minutes, or until the nuts begin to brown and emit a nutty aroma, stirring occasionally. Stir in the ras el hanout, toss in the dates and dried apricots, and cook, stirring, for 2 minutes. Fluff up the couscous using a fork, then transfer to the pan, mix well, and heat through. Remove from the heat.

4. Pile the couscous onto a serving plate in a mound. Sprinkle the cinnamon through your fingers to create vertical lines from the top of the mound to the bottom, like the spokes of a wheel. Serve immediately.

GRATIN OF
GREEN CHILES
WITH CREAM & CHEESE

| SERVES: 4–6 | PREP TIME: 20–25 mins, plus standing | COOK TIME: 25 mins |

THE TRULY DELICIOUS COMBINATION OF PEPPERY, LEMONY CHILES AND SWEET, RICH CREAM OFFERS THE PERFECT BALANCE OF TEXTURE AND FLAVOR.

INGREDIENTS

1½ pounds thin-fleshed, mild green chiles, preferably Anaheim

1 cup light cream

1 cup heavy cream

1½ cups crumbled feta cheese or queso paisa cheese

salt and pepper (optional)

soft cornmeal tortillas, to serve

1. Wipe the chiles, but don't remove the stems or seeds. Using tongs, hold the chiles over a gas flame, or cook under a preheated broiler or oven on the highest setting, until the skins are black and blistered in places. Transfer to a plastic or paper bag and let stand for 10 minutes to loosen the skins. Remove the skins. Slice the flesh into ribbons and arrange in a gratin dish.

2. Meanwhile, heat all the cream in a small saucepan and remove it as soon as it reaches boiling point. Pour it over the chile ribbons and sprinkle with the cheese. Season with a little salt and pepper—not too much, because the cheese may already be salty and one or two of the chiles may be hot.

3. Preheat the broiler to high. Cook the chiles for 8–10 minutes, or until brown and bubbling. Meanwhile, wrap the tortillas in aluminum foil and warm through in a preheated low oven for 5 minutes. Serve the gratin piping hot, with the warm tortillas for mopping up.

SWEET POTATO & BROCCOLI BURGERS

| MAKES: 4–6 | PREP TIME: 10–12 mins, plus chilling | COOK TIME: 45–50 mins |

THERE ARE A LOT OF INTERESTING TEXTURES AND FLAVORS VYING FOR YOUR ATTENTION IN THESE TASTY VEGETARIAN BURGERS.

INGREDIENTS

salt for cooking the sweet potatoes

3 sweet potatoes, cut into chunks

2½ cups broccoli florets

2–3 garlic cloves, crushed

1 red onion, finely chopped or grated

1½–2 fresh red jalapeño chiles, seeded and finely chopped

1½ cups shredded halloumi cheese or quesco paiso cheese

2 tablespoons whole-wheat flour

2–3 tablespoons sunflower oil

3 onions, sliced

1 tablespoon chopped fresh cilantro

salt and pepper (optional)

1. Bring a saucepan of lightly salted water to a boil, add the sweet potatoes, bring back to a boil, and cook for 15–20 minutes, or until tender. Drain and mash. Bring a separate small saucepan of lightly salted water to a boil, add the broccoli, bring back to a boil, and cook for 3 minutes, then drain and plunge into cold water. Drain again, then add to the mashed sweet potato.

2. Stir in the garlic, red onion, chiles, cheese, and salt and pepper, if using. Mix well and shape into four to six equal patties, then coat in the flour. Cover and let chill in the refrigerator for at least 1 hour.

3. Heat 1½ tablespoons of the oil in a heavy skillet. Add the sliced onions and sauté over medium heat for 12–15 minutes, or until soft. Stir in the cilantro and reserve.

4. Preheat the barbecue or broiler. Brush the patties with the remaining oil and cook over medium heat for 5–6 minutes on each side, or until cooked through.

5. Top the burgers with the reserved fried onions and cilantro and serve immediately.

VEGETABLE CHILI

SERVES: 4	PREP TIME: 35 mins	COOK TIME: 1 hr 20 mins

THIS DELICIOUS, SPICY VEGETARIAN CHILI IS FULL OF VEGETABLES, BEANS, AND WONDERFUL FLAVORS. YOU CAN INCREASE THE AMOUNT OF CHILI POWDER AND CUMIN IF YOU WANT TO INCREASE THE HEAT FACTOR.

INGREDIENTS

1 eggplant, cut into 1-inch slices

2 tablespoons olive oil

1 large red onion, finely chopped

2 red or yellow bell peppers, seeded and finely chopped

3-4 garlic cloves, finely chopped

1 (28-ounce) can diced tomatoes

1 tablespoon mild chili powder

½ teaspoon ground cumin

½ teaspoon dried oregano

2 small zucchini, quartered lengthwise and sliced

1 (15-ounce) can kidney beans, drained and rinsed

2 cups water

1 tablespoon tomato paste

6 scallions, finely chopped

1 cup shredded cheddar cheese, for sprinkling

salt and pepper (optional)

1. Brush the eggplant slices on one side with oil. Heat half the remaining oil in a large, heavy skillet over medium–high heat. Add the eggplant slices, oiled side up, and cook for 5–6 minutes, or until brown on one side. Turn the slices over, cook on the other side until brown, and transfer to a plate. Cut into bite-size pieces.

2. Heat the remaining oil in a large saucepan over medium heat. Add the onion and red bell peppers and cook, stirring occasionally, for 3–4 minutes, or until the onion is soft but not brown.

3. Add the garlic and cook for an additional 2–3 minutes, or until the onion is beginning to brown.

4. Add the tomatoes, chili powder, cumin, and oregano. Season with salt and pepper, if using. Bring just to a boil, reduce the heat, cover, and simmer gently for 15 minutes.

5. Add the zucchini, eggplant pieces, and beans. Stir in the water and the tomato paste. Bring back to a boil, then cover and continue simmering for 45 minutes, or until the vegetables are tender. Add salt and pepper, if using. Ladle into serving bowls, top with the scallions, and sprinkle with the cheese. Serve.

CHILI SAUCES
AROUND THE WORLD

Although chiles originated in South and Central America, they are now grown in just about every part of the world—and are a key part of the many hot and spicy flavors associated with particular regions.

South America

The home of the chile produces a traditionally mild cuisine—so the addition of a sauce is often needed to add a little fire, although even the hot sauces tend to focus on flavor rather than heat. The most popular remains adobo sauce, made from chiles such as chipotle, with Mexican oregano, onions, and tomatoes; but all amateur chefs will have their own recipe, often using chipotle or jalapeño chiles.

United States

Our hot sauces are made with chiles, vinegar, and salt, but often with the addition of fruits and vegetables as diverse as raspberries, mangoes, tomatoes, and carrots to mellow out the flavor or add a thick edge to the sauce. The most popular chiles used in American sauces are jalapeño, chipotle, habanero, and cayenne, and the results range from very mild barbecue sauces to the spicy hot pepper sauce.

Caribbean

Sauces made from chiles feature heavily in Caribbean cuisine and, like their American cousins, most are made with the addition of fruit and vegetables to temper the flavor. However, most Caribbean sauces feature habanero and Scotch bonnet chiles, so the results still tend to be much hotter. Homemade sauces are common, with onions and garlic often added for extra piquancy.

Europe

Believe it or not, two of the hottest chili sauces in the world originate from Great Britain. Made from the naga viper and infinity chiles, they remain a specialized taste. However, the Portuguese peri-peri sauce, made from crushed peri-peri chiles with lime, citrus peel, garlic, and various herbs, remains popular across the continent.

Middle East

The ancients of this region believed that chiles held near-magical healing powers, and so much of the traditional cuisine features sauces with chiles as ingredients. The most popular remains harissa—made from fresh and dried hot chiles blended into a thick paste with garlic, olive oil, and spices, such as caraway seeds. Other examples are *shatta*, used in Levantine cuisine, made with chiles and olive oil, and *skhug* from Yemen and Israel.

Asia

Chili sauces are used widely in Asia. Often made with the addition of beans, many sauces are made as a thick paste, which can be added to curries (or stews), as a dipping sauce, or for stir-frying. India is one of the largest chile producers and they define the experience of many of the dishes (see jwala chiles, opposite, left). Specific Asian sauces include the Chinese Lao Gan Ma, combining chiles with soybean paste, and the Korean gochujang, made with chile, glutinous rice, fermented soybeans, and salt. Thailand is known for its sriracha sauce, as used in Salmon Satay with Sriracha Sauce (opposite, right), as well as its spicy dipping sauces (nam chim) and fish sauces (nam pla). Sambal is a chili sauce from Indonesia, Malaysia, and Sri Lanka that has developed an international appeal.

BUTTERNUT SQUASH
LINGUINE WITH
ARRABBIATA SAUCE

SERVES: 2	PREP TIME: 15 mins	COOK TIME: 20 mins

PASTA IS A POPULAR FAVORITE, BUT OCCASIONALLY IT'S GREAT TO TRY SOMETHING DIFFERENT. VEGETABLES PREPARED SO THEY LOOK A LOT LIKE SPAGHETTI TASTE GREAT, AND THEY ARE ALSO LOW IN CARBS.

INGREDIENTS

1 butternut squash

8 sprays cooking oil spray

2 tablespoons chopped fresh flat-leaf parsley, to garnish

ARRABBIATA SAUCE

1 tablespoon olive oil

1 onion, chopped

2 garlic cloves, crushed

1 red chile, seeded and finely chopped

3 tablespoons red wine

1 teaspoon sugar

1 teaspoon crushed red pepper flakes

2 teaspoons red pesto

¾ cup canned chopped tomatoes

4 anchovy fillets from a jar, drained

8 black olives, pitted and coarsely chopped

1 teaspoon dried Italian seasoning

½ teaspoon salt

½ teaspoon pepper

1. Cut the bulbous end off the squash and set aside for another recipe. Cut the stem off the squash and discard. Peel the remaining squash. If you are using a spiralizer, cut the squash into two chunks and put each chunk through the spiralizer. If you are using a julienne peeler, set the squash on a stable work surface and slice off julienne strips.

2. To make the arrabbiata sauce, put a large saucepan over medium-low heat and add the oil. Add the onion and sauté for 8 minutes, or until soft and transparent. Add the garlic and chile and stir for 1 minute. Add the wine, sugar, crushed red pepper flakes, pesto, tomatoes, anchovies, olives, Italian seasoning, salt, and pepper and simmer for 20 minutes.

3. Meanwhile, preheat the oven to 375°F. Put the squash spaghetti on a large baking pan and spray with the cooking oil spray. Bake in the preheated oven for 6 minutes, and then turn the spaghetti over using tongs. Bake for an additional 4 minutes, or until the strands are just tender with the occasional tinge of gold.

4. Transfer the spaghetti to two warm serving plates. Spoon the arrabbiata sauce over the spaghetti, garnish with the parsley, and serve immediately.

CELERIAC, FENNEL & PEACH SLAW

SERVES: 4	PREP TIME: 10 mins	COOK TIME: none

A GOOD SLAW, THIS ONE SPICED UP WITH SRIRACHA CHILI SAUCE, CAN BE USED IN MANY WAYS: AS A QUICK SNACK, AS A SANDWICH OR WRAP COMPONENT, OR SERVED WITH COLD MEAT AND A CRISPY SALAD.

INGREDIENTS

¼ cup mayonnaise

1 teaspoon sriracha chili sauce

1 teaspoon horseradish sauce

zest and juice of 1 lemon

½ teaspoon pepper

2 ripe peaches, pitted and sliced

⅓ celeriac, cut into matchsticks

1 fennel bulb, sliced

1 small red onion, sliced

1. In a large bowl, whisk together the mayonnaise, chili sauce, horseradish sauce, lemon zest and juice, and pepper.

2. Add the peaches, celeriac, fennel, and onion to the bowl.

3. Mix well to combine thoroughly, then serve immediately.

TIP

THIS SLAW WILL WORK WELL WITH ANY STONE FRUIT AND IS GREAT SERVED WITH PORK, CHICKEN, OR FISH.

SMOKY BBQ
BEANS

SERVES: 4	PREP TIME: 10 mins	COOK TIME: 30 mins

THE CANNELLINI BEANS IN THIS RECIPE ARE INFUSED WITH DEEP-SEATED, SMOKY FLAVORS, AND THE FINAL DISH COMBINES THESE TENDER, CREAMY BEANS WITH AN ADDICTIVE BARBECUE FLAVOR.

INGREDIENTS

¼ cup olive oil

1 large onion, chopped

2 garlic cloves, chopped

2 celery stalks, chopped

1 large carrot, chopped

1 teaspoon fennel seeds

2 teaspoons dried oregano

2 teaspoons smoked paprika

1 tablespoon chipotle chile paste

1 tablespoon molasses

2 cups tomato puree or tomato sauce

1 (15-ounce) can cannellini beans, drained and rinsed

salt and pepper (optional)

1. Heat the oil in a large saucepan over medium heat. Add the onion, garlic, celery, and carrot, cover with a lid, and let cook for 15 minutes, or until translucent and soft.

2. Add the fennel seeds, oregano, paprika, chile paste, and molasses. Cook for 5 minutes, until the sugars start to caramelize.

3. Add the tomato puree or sauce and beans and cook for an additional 10 minutes.

4. Season with salt and pepper, if using, and serve.

TIP

FOR THE CARNIVORE IN YOUR LIFE, TRY ADDING CHOPPED SMOKED BACON, CHORIZO, OR FRANKFURTERS TO THE BEANS.

SPICY MASHED
EGGPLANT

SERVES: 4	**PREP TIME:** 15–20 mins	**COOK TIME:** 45–55 mins

THIS VERSION OF BAINGAN KA BHARTA HAS ITS ORIGINS IN THE PUNJAB. BHARTAS ARE LARGELY NORTH INDIAN IN ORIGIN AND CAN BE MADE FROM ALL KINDS OF VEGETABLES.

INGREDIENTS

4 large eggplant
2 tablespoons vegetable oil or peanut oil
4 tablespoons butter
2 onions, finely chopped
2 teaspoons grated fresh ginger
4 garlic cloves, crushed
2 fresh green chiles, finely sliced
3 tomatoes, finely chopped
2 teaspoons salt
1 teaspoon chili powder
1 teaspoon smoked paprika
2 teaspoons ground coriander
1 teaspoon ground cumin
1 teaspoon ground turmeric
½ teaspoon garam masala
⅓ cup finely chopped fresh cilantro

1. Prick each eggplant all over with a fork and roast them over an open flame (if you have a gas stove-top) or under a medium-hot broiler, turning them from time to time, for 20–25 minutes, until the skin blackens and chars. To check if an eggplant is cooked, press the back of a spoon into the skin; if it enters the eggplant like soft butter, it is done. Let cool.

2. When the eggplant is cool enough to handle, remove the skins and coarsely mash the pulp. Set aside.

3. Heat the oil and butter in a large, nonstick skillet and add the onions. Sauté for 5–6 minutes, until soft. Add the ginger, garlic, and chiles and stir-fry for 1–2 minutes.

4. Stir in the tomatoes and salt and cook for 12–15 minutes. Add the chili powder, paprika, ground coriander, cumin, and turmeric.

5. Stir in the reserved eggplant flesh and cook for 3–4 minutes. Stir in the garam masala and fresh cilantro. Serve immediately.

THAI RED FRIES

SERVES: 4	PREP TIME: 15 mins	COOK TIME: 30 mins

THESE UNUSUAL OVEN-BAKED FRIES HIT ALL THE RIGHT TASTE BUDS— SWEET, SPICY, TANGY, SALTY, AND ALL-ROUND DELICIOUS.

INGREDIENTS

3 tablespoons vegetable oil

2 tablespoons packed light brown sugar

2 tablespoons Thai fish sauce

2 tablespoons lime juice

1 tablespoon Thai red curry paste

½ teaspoon cayenne pepper

8 potatoes (about 2 pounds)

CILANTRO KETCHUP

1 garlic clove

⅓ cup fresh cilantro

1 cup ketchup

2 tablespoons lime juice

1. Preheat the oven to 450°F. Grease a large baking sheet with 1 tablespoon of the oil.

2. Put the remaining oil, sugar, fish sauce, lime juice, curry paste, and cayenne pepper into a mixing bowl and stir together until well combined.

3. Peel the potatoes, if desired, and cut them into ¼ x ¼-inch sticks. Add them to the mixture in the bowl and toss to coat. Let stand for about 5 minutes, then, using a slotted spoon, transfer the potatoes to the prepared baking sheet, letting the excess marinade run off into the bowl. Spread the potatoes in a single layer. Bake in the preheated oven for 25–30 minutes, turning after about 15 minutes, until brown and crisp.

4. Meanwhile, to make the ketchup, chop the garlic and cilantro in a food processor. Add the ketchup and lime juice and process until well combined. Transfer to a serving bowl.

5. Serve the fries hot with the ketchup for dipping.

MEAT & POULTRY MAINS

When it's a sizzling, spice-packed meaty main that's needed, these dishes won't disappoint. Choose from chicken, turkey, beef, pork, or lamb, and impress your family and friends with Goan Spiced Chicken; Hot Sesame Beef; Turkey Stir-Fry with Spiced Coffee Glaze; Pork with Chiles, Vinegar & Garlic; or treat yourself to a Colossal Lamb Kabob with Hot Chili Sauce.

GOAN
SPICED CHICKEN

| SERVES: 4 | PREP TIME: 20 mins | COOK TIME: 35–40 mins |

THIS CLASSIC, SPICY CHICKEN DISH FROM THE SHORES OF GOA IS A LOCAL FAVORITE. MADE FROM A BLEND OF COCONUT MILK, RED CHILES, AND AROMATIC SPICES, IT IS BEST SERVED WITH STEAMED RICE AND MANGO CHUTNEY.

INGREDIENTS

6 black peppercorns
3 cloves
2 teaspoons fennel seeds
4 dried red chiles
1 teaspoon cardamom seeds
2 teaspoons white poppy seeds
2 cinnamon sticks
2 teaspoons salt
1 teaspoon ground turmeric
1 teaspoon ground cumin
1 teaspoon ground coriander
¼ cup vegetable oil or peanut oil
1 onion, minced
3 garlic cloves, crushed
1¼ pounds skinless, boneless chicken thighs, cut into bite-size pieces
1¼ cups coconut milk
1¼ cups cold water
1 teaspoon tamarind paste

1. Put a large, nonstick skillet over medium heat and add the peppercorns, cloves, fennel seeds, dried red chiles, cardamom seeds, white poppy seeds, and cinnamon sticks. Dry-fry for 1–2 minutes, then remove from the heat and let cool.

2. Put the cooled whole spices into a spice grinder with the salt, turmeric, cumin, and ground coriander. Process until ground to a fairly fine powder.

3. Heat the oil in a large saucepan, add the onion and garlic, and sauté over medium heat for 2–3 minutes. Increase the heat to high, add the chicken, and stir-fry for 5–6 minutes, or until sealed.

4. Add the spice mixture and stir-fry for 1–2 minutes, then add the coconut milk and water. Bring to a boil, then reduce the heat to low–medium and simmer gently for 15–20 minutes. Stir in the tamarind paste and cook for an additional 2–3 minutes, or until the chicken is cooked through and tender, with no sign of pink when the thickest part is pierced with the tip of a sharp knife. Serve immediately.

SPICY HAMBURGERS WITH GUACAMOLE & WEDGES

SERVES: 4	PREP TIME: 1 hr	COOK TIME: 15 mins

A GOOD HAMBURGER IS HARD TO BEAT, AND IF YOU MAKE YOUR OWN, YOU'LL KNOW WHAT IS IN IT AND WHERE THE MEAT HAS COME FROM.

INGREDIENTS

1 pound sirloin steak, visible fat removed, diced

½ teaspoon chili powder

2 teaspoons cumin seeds, coarsely crushed

1 tablespoon fresh thyme leaves

4 baking potatoes, unpeeled, scrubbed, and cut into wedges

3 tablespoons virgin olive oil

1 teaspoon paprika

sea salt and pepper (optional)

GUACAMOLE

1 large avocado, pitted and peeled

juice of 1 lime

2 scallions, finely chopped

TO SERVE

4 spelt burger buns, halved

1 romaine or cos lettuce heart, shredded

handful of arugula leaves

2 large tomatoes, sliced

1. Preheat the oven to 400°F. With the motor running on a food processor, drop in a few pieces of steak at a time, until it is all coarsely chopped. Alternatively, press the pieces through a grinder on the coarse setting.

2. Put the chili powder, half the cumin seeds, half the thyme, and a little salt and pepper, if using, in a bowl and mix well. Rub the mixture into the steak, then shape the mixture into four patties. Cover and chill in the refrigerator for 15 minutes.

3. Bring a saucepan of water to a boil, add the potato wedges, and cook for 4–5 minutes. Drain well and transfer to a roasting pan. Drizzle the wedges with 2 tablespoons of oil, then turn them until they are well coated. Sprinkle with the paprika, the remaining cumin and thyme, and a little salt and pepper, if using. Bake, turning once, for 25–30 minutes, or until golden brown.

4. For the guacamole, put the avocado into a shallow bowl and mash with a fork. Add the lime juice and scallions, season with a little salt and pepper, if using, and mix well.

5. Preheat the broiler to medium-high. Brush the burgers with a little of the remaining oil, then cook, turning halfway through, for 8–10 minutes, or a little less for those who like their burgers pink in the middle. Let stand for a few minutes. Meanwhile, toast the buns, then stack the lettuce, arugula, tomatoes, the hot patties, and a spoonful of guacamole on the bottoms and add the bun lids. Serve with the wedges.

TURKEY STIR-FRY
WITH SPICED COFFEE GLAZE

SERVES: 4	PREP TIME: 25 mins, plus marinating	COOK TIME: 15 mins

THIS TEMPTING, FLAVORSOME STIR-FRY REQUIRES ONLY FIFTEEN MINUTES COOKING, AND IT WILL UNDOUBTEDLY SPICE UP YOUR DAY.

INGREDIENTS

1 pound turkey breast, sliced into thin strips

1 teaspoon finely grated fresh ginger

2 garlic cloves, crushed

1 teaspoon five-spice paste

4 teaspoons sesame oil

¼ cup strong black coffee, cooled

¼ cup teriyaki sauce

2 tablespoons honey

2 tablespoons rice wine vinegar

2 teaspoons cornstarch

6 scallions, trimmed and sliced

1 red bell pepper, seeded and thinly sliced

1 yellow bell pepper, seeded and thinly sliced

salt and pepper (optional)

1 pound cooked egg noodles, to serve

1. Put the turkey into a shallow, nonmetallic bowl and add the ginger, garlic, five-spice paste, and half the oil. Stir well, then cover and let marinate at room temperature for 1 hour.

2. Mix together the coffee, teriyaki sauce, honey, vinegar, and cornstarch in a small bowl. Cover and set aside.

3. Heat the remaining oil in a large wok until almost smoking. Remove the turkey from the marinade, add to the wok, and stir-fry over high heat for 3–4 minutes, until brown. Add the scallions, red bell pepper, and yellow bell pepper and stir-fry for an additional 1–2 minutes.

4. Pour in the coffee mixture and stir-fry for an additional 1–2 minutes, until the sauce has thickened and coated the turkey and vegetables. Serve with the noodles.

HOT SESAME BEEF

SERVES: 4	PREP TIME: 20 mins	COOK TIME: 10 mins

THIS SESAME BEEF IS BEAUTIFULLY SUCCULENT AND STICKY, WITH THE BEEF AND VEGETABLES BATHED IN A SPICY SAUCE OF BEEF BROTH, SOY SAUCE, GINGER, GARLIC, AND CRUSHED RED PEPPER FLAKES.

INGREDIENTS

1 pound tenderloin steak, cut into thin strips

1½ tablespoons sesame seeds

½ cup beef broth or stock

2 tablespoons soy sauce

2 tablespoons grated fresh ginger

2 garlic cloves, finely chopped

1 teaspoon cornstarch

½ teaspoon crushed red pepper flakes

3 tablespoons sesame oil

1 large head of broccoli, cut into florets

1 yellow bell pepper, seeded and thinly sliced

1 fresh red chile, finely sliced

1 tablespoon chili oil, or to taste

wild rice, to serve

1. Mix the beef strips with 1 tablespoon of the sesame seeds in a small bowl.

2. In a separate bowl, stir together the broth or stock, soy sauce, ginger, garlic, cornstarch, and red pepper flakes.

3. Heat 1 tablespoon of the sesame oil in a large wok. Add the beef strips and stir-fry for 2–3 minutes. Remove and set aside, then wipe out the wok with paper towels.

4. Heat the remaining sesame oil in the wok, add the broccoli, yellow bell pepper, red chile, and chili oil and stir-fry for 2–3 minutes.

5. Stir in the broth mixture, cover, and simmer for 2 minutes.

6. Return the beef to the wok and simmer until the juices thicken, stirring occasionally. Cook for an additional 1–2 minutes. Sprinkle with the remaining sesame seeds and serve over wild rice.

SPICY FRIED CHICKEN
WITH RED CABBAGE &
CHILE COLESLAW

SERVES: 4	PREP TIME: 20 mins, plus marinating	COOK TIME: 35 mins

INSTEAD OF THE USUAL BREAD CRUMBS, THIS CHICKEN HAS A CRUNCHY COATING OF CORNMEAL, QUINOA FLOUR, AND WHOLE-WHEAT FLOUR, WHICH WORKS EXCELLENTLY WITH THE ZINGY FLAVORS OF THE COLESLAW.

INGREDIENTS

1 cup sour cream

½ teaspoon cayenne pepper

1 garlic clove, crushed

4 chicken thighs and
4 chicken drumsticks
(about 1¾ pounds)

2 teaspoons coarse cornmeal

2 tablespoons quinoa flour

2 tablespoons whole-wheat flour

vegetable oil, for deep-frying

sea salt and pepper (optional)

COLESLAW

2 cups shredded red cabbage

4 cups shredded fennel

1 red chile, seeded and thinly sliced
lengthwise

½ cup Greek-style plain yogurt

juice of ¼ lemon

1. Put the sour cream, cayenne, and garlic into a large bowl and season well with salt and pepper, if using. Add the chicken and toss well. Cover the bowl with plastic wrap and chill in the refrigerator for 2–3 hours, or overnight if you have time.

2. To make the coleslaw, put all the ingredients into a large bowl and toss well, then season with salt and pepper, if using. Cover and chill in the refrigerator.

3. Mix together the cornmeal and flours on a plate and season with salt and pepper, if using. Heat a heavy skillet filled halfway with oil over medium-high heat to 350°F, or until a cube of bread browns in 30 seconds. While it heats, sprinkle the flour mixture over the chicken.

4. Cook the chicken in two batches, because too much chicken in the pan will make the oil temperature drop. Using tongs, carefully place half the chicken in the oil. Cook for 6–8 minutes, then turn and cook for an additional 6–8 minutes, until the coating is a deep golden brown, the chicken is cooked through to the bone, and the juices run clear with no sign of pink when the tip of a sharp knife is inserted into the thickest part of the meat.

5. Using a slotted spoon, transfer the cooked chicken to paper towels to drain, then keep warm in a low oven while you cook the second batch.

6. Serve the chicken on a sharing board with the coleslaw.

THAI GREEN
CHICKEN CURRY
& UDON NOODLES

SERVES: 4	PREP TIME: 10 mins	COOK TIME: 15 mins

THAI "GREEN" CURRY IS SO CHRISTENED BECAUSE OF THE GREEN CHILES FROM WHICH IT IS PREPARED—GREEN CURRY PASTE IS USED IN THIS FRAGRANT, CREAMY CURRY AND THE ONE-TO-THREE-TEASPOON OPTION MEANS THAT YOU CAN CALM DOWN OR ACCENTUATE THE HEAT TO YOUR TASTE.

INGREDIENTS

1 tablespoon vegetable oil

1 shallot, diced

1–3 teaspoons Thai green curry paste

1 (13½-ounce) can coconut milk

1 tablespoon Thai fish sauce

juice of 1 lime

1 tablespoon packed light brown sugar

⅔ cup fresh basil leaves

⅔ cup fresh cilantro leaves

1 pound fresh udon noodles

2⅓ cups shredded cooked chicken

3 scallions, thinly sliced, to garnish

1. Heat the oil in a nonstick skillet over medium heat. Add the shallot and cook for 5 minutes, until soft. Add the curry paste and cook, stirring, for 1 minute.

2. Scoop off the thick cream in the can that will have risen to the top of the coconut milk. Add the cream to the pan with the fish sauce, lime juice, and sugar. Cook, stirring frequently, for 1–2 minutes. Stir in the remaining coconut milk and bring the mixture to a boil. Reduce the heat to low and simmer, stirring occasionally, for an additional 5 minutes, or until the sauce thickens. Remove from the heat and let cool slightly. Add the basil and cilantro.

3. Transfer the mixture to a food processor, add the basil and cilantro to a food processor and process until smooth and bright green. Return the sauce to the pan and reheat over medium–low heat.

4. Cook the noodles according to the package directions and place them in a large serving bowl.

5. Add the chicken and sauce to the noodles and toss to combine. Serve immediately, garnished with the scallions.

WHOLE TANDOORI CHICKEN

| SERVES: 4 | PREP TIME: 35 mins, plus marinating | COOK TIME: 55 mins |

THIS DISH ORIGINATES IN THE PUNJAB. THE "TANDOORI" IN THE NAME COMES FROM THE TANDOOR, A CYLINDRICAL CLAY OVEN, WHERE THIS CHICKEN DISH IS TRADITIONALLY PREPARED AT AN EXTREMELY HIGH TEMPERATURE.

INGREDIENTS

1 (3¼-pound) chicken
2 teaspoons garam masala
1¼ cups plain yogurt
1 onion, finely chopped
2 garlic cloves, crushed
1-inch piece fresh ginger, peeled and grated
juice of 1 lemon
2 tablespoons tomato paste
1 teaspoon chili powder
1 teaspoon ground cumin
1 teaspoon ground turmeric
1 tablespoon paprika (not smoked)
1 teaspoon salt

TO SERVE
basmati rice
naan or other flatbread
lime wedges
hot lime pickle

1. Cut two slits into each chicken leg and two into each thigh. They should just reach the bone. Make two shallower cuts into the fleshiest part of each breast. These are to let the marinade penetrate into the meat.

2. Mix all of the remaining ingredients together in a food processor and blend to a smooth paste. Put the chicken into a large, nonmetallic dish and cover it in the paste, massaging it deep into the skin and flesh. Place the chicken, uncovered, in the refrigerator to marinate for as long as possible—preferably 24 hours.

3. Remove the chicken from the refrigerator before cooking to bring it to room temperature. Preheat the oven to 425°F. Put the chicken into the oven and cook, uncovered, for 20 minutes, then reduce the heat to 350°F. Baste the chicken and cook for another 35 minutes. When fully cooked the juices will run clear when the tip of a sharp knife is inserted into the thickest part of the meat. Turn off the oven and open the door, but keep the chicken inside to rest for 20 minutes. Serve with rice, naan, lime wedges, and lime pickle.

SPICY RICE WITH CHICKEN & POMEGRANATE

SERVES: 4	PREP TIME: 25 mins	COOK TIME: 1 hr

SPICE UP YOUR LUNCH WITH THIS TEMPTING CHICKEN-AND-RICE DISH, FINISHED WITH FLESHY, PINK POMEGRANATE SEEDS, WHICH PACK A POWERFUL NUTRIENT PUNCH, PLUS VIVID, GREEN, ANTIOXIDANT-RICH FRESH HERBS.

INGREDIENTS

4 large chicken thighs
2 teaspoons five-spice powder
2 tablespoons olive oil
2 red onions, finely sliced
2 garlic cloves, finely sliced
5 cardamom pods, crushed
2 star anise
1¼ cups brown rice
3 cups vegetable broth or stock
⅔ cup coarsely chopped fresh mint
½ cup coarsely chopped fresh flat-leaf parsley
seeds of 1 small pomegranate
¼ cup toasted almonds
finely grated zest and juice of 1 lemon
salt and pepper (optional)

1. Preheat the oven to 400°F. Put the chicken thighs onto a baking pan and sprinkle with the five-spice powder. Drizzle with 1 tablespoon of olive oil and roast in the preheated oven for 20 minutes, or until the juices run clear when the thickest part of the meat is pierced and no traces of pink remain in the center. Remove from the oven and set aside to cool.

2. Meanwhile, heat the remaining tablespoon of olive oil in a large saucepan over medium–low heat. Add the onion and gently sauté for 10–12 minutes, or until soft and starting to caramelize. Stir in the garlic, cardamom pods, and star anise and cook for an additional minute. Add the rice and stir well.

3. Pour in the broth or stock and bring the pan to a boil. Cover and simmer gently for 25–30 minutes, or until all the broth has been absorbed and the rice is tender.

4. Once the chicken is cool enough to handle, remove the meat from the bones and finely slice. Add to the rice mixture, with any remaining juices, and season with salt and pepper, if using.

5. Stir in half of the mint and parsley. Top with the remaining herbs, pomegranate seeds, toasted almonds, lemon juice, and zest and serve immediately.

SPICES FROM
DRIED FRUITS & SEEDS

A spice is "a seed, fruit, root, bark, berry, bud, or other vegetable substance used for flavoring, coloring, or preserving." Chile is classed as a spice, but there are many others from which to choose.

The spice trade was a significant driving force within the world economy from the end of the Middle Ages, with the most common and popular spices in the medieval period including black pepper (the most expensive), cinnamon, cumin, nutmeg, ginger, and cloves. Spices can be created from different plant forms—from dried fruits or seeds, such as mustard, nutmeg, fennel, and black pepper; arils, such as mace; barks, such as cassia and cinnamon; dried flower buds, such as cloves; stigmas, such as saffron; and roots, such as turmeric and ginger. Here, we look at spices that are sourced from dried fruits or seeds.

Allspice, also called pimento, is an aromatic spice created from the dried unripe berry of the West Indian allspice tree. It was called "allspice" because it was felt to capture the flavors of cinnamon, nutmeg, and cloves. It is used widely in Caribbean cuisine, especially in jerk seasoning, and in mole sauces.

Black pepper is the dried fruit of a flowering vine in the *Piperaceae* family and peppercorns are a familiar feature in every kitchen. First grown in southern India, it is commonly used to enhance the appetite and give dishes a warming quality.

Cayenne pepper is from the chile family, and the dried fruit is commonly used in its powdered form after the peppers are dried and ground and sifted to create the powder that gives heat to spicy dishes.

Cumin seeds are small seeds, similar in size to rice grains, taken from the plant *Cuminum cyminum*. They have a warm and slightly bitter quality and are used widely in South Asian, North African, and Latin American cuisines. Cumin is available in whole and ground form.

Fennel is a dried, oval-shaped seed that comes from the herb *Foeniculum vulgare*, which is distinctive for its licorice flavor (see opposite, above right). Fennel seeds can be brown or green—green seeds are the best choice for cooking.

Mustard seeds are the fruit pods of the mustard plant and are available as black, brown, yellow, or white seeds. They have a nutty taste and are used extensively in Indian cooking.

Nutmeg is the seed of the nutmeg tree, *Myristica fragrans* (see opposite, below), which is indigenous to the Spice Islands in Indonesia. It has a comforting spicy warmth and is usually used in powdered form. It is equally useful in sweet and savory dishes.

Paprika originated in central Mexico and is made from the air-dried fruits of the chile pepper, which are then formed into a powder. Bright red, it is often used to add color to dishes. It is available in different strengths, but is milder than cayenne pepper, and has a sweet quality.

Star anise is the dried fruit of an evergreen tree called *Illicium velum* that is native to southwest China (see opposite, above left). It has a distinctive eight-point star shape and contains anethole, an oil with a licorice flavor. It is widely used in Chinese and Indian cuisine.

MEXICAN TURKEY BURGERS

| SERVES: 4 | PREP TIME: 25 mins, plus chilling | COOK TIME: 20 mins |

THESE DELICIOUS ROAST BURGERS ARE IDEAL FOR A BARBECUE, OR CAN EASILY BE PREPARED IN THE KITCHEN TO GIVE A BARBECUE FLAVOR TO AN INDOOR MEAL.

INGREDIENTS

1 pound ground fresh turkey

¾ cup canned refried beans

2–4 garlic cloves, crushed

1–2 fresh jalapeño chiles, seeded and finely chopped

2 tablespoons tomato paste

1 tablespoon chopped fresh cilantro

1 tablespoon sunflower oil

salt and pepper

shredded baby spinach leaves

TO SERVE

4 cheese-topped burger buns, halved

salsa

guacamole

tortilla chips

1. Put the ground turkey in a bowl and break up any large lumps. Beat the refried beans until smooth, then add them to the turkey in the bowl.

2. Add the garlic, chiles, tomato paste, and cilantro with salt and pepper to taste and mix together. Shape into four equal patties, then cover and let chill in the refrigerator for 1 hour.

3. Preheat the barbecue, if using. Otherwise, add the oil to a large skillet over medium–high heat, until hot. Add the patties and cook for 5–6 minutes on each side, or until browned and cooked through. If barbecuing, brush the patties with the oil and cook over medium-hot coals for 5–6 minutes on each side, or until cooked through.

4. Place the spinach on the bottom halves of the burger buns and top with the burgers. Spoon over a little salsa and guacamole and top with the lids. Serve immediately with tortilla chips on the side.

SPICED TURKEY STEW
WITH WHOLE-GRAIN COUSCOUS

SERVES: 4	PREP TIME: 20 mins	COOK TIME: 25 mins

CAPTURE THE FLAVORS OF MIDDLE EASTERN COOKING WITH THIS EASY, LIGHTLY SPICED STOVE-TOP TURKEY STEW.

INGREDIENTS

1 tablespoon virgin olive oil

1 pound skinless and boneless turkey breast, cut into ¾-inch pieces

1 onion, coarsely chopped

2 garlic cloves, finely chopped

1 red bell pepper, seeded and coarsely chopped

1 orange pepper, seeded and coarsely chopped

4 tomatoes, coarsely chopped

1 teaspoon cumin seeds, coarsely crushed

1 teaspoon paprika

zest and juice of 1 unwaxed lemon

sea salt and pepper (optional)

TO SERVE

1⅓ cups whole-grain Israeli couscous or pearl couscous

2 tablespoons coarsely chopped fresh flat-leaf parsley

2 tablespoons coarsely chopped fresh cilantro

1. Heat the oil in a large skillet over medium heat. Add the turkey, a few pieces at a time, then add the onion. Sauté, stirring, for 5 minutes, or until the turkey is golden.

2. Add the garlic, red and orange bell peppers, and tomatoes, then stir in the cumin seeds and paprika. Add the lemon juice and season with salt and pepper, if using. Stir well, then cover and cook, stirring from time to time, for 20 minutes, or until the tomatoes have formed a thick sauce and the turkey is cooked through and the juices run clear with no sign of pink when a piece is cut in half.

3. Meanwhile, fill a saucepan halfway with water and bring to a boil. Add the couscous and cook according to the package directions, or until just tender. Transfer to a strainer and drain well.

4. Spoon the couscous onto plates and top with the turkey stew. Mix the parsley and cilantro with the lemon zest, then sprinkle with the stew and serve.

PORK WITH CHILES, VINEGAR & GARLIC

SERVES: 4	PREP TIME: 10 mins, plus chilling	COOK TIME: 1¼–1½ hrs

WHEN THE PORTUGUESE TRAVELED TO INDIA, THEY TOOK PORK PRESERVED IN VINEGAR, GARLIC, AND PEPPER, WHICH WAS SPICED UP TO SUIT INDIAN TASTES, AND THIS VINDALOO DISH WAS BORN.

INGREDIENTS

2–6 dried red chiles, torn

5 cloves

1-inch piece cinnamon stick, broken up

4 green cardamom pods

½ teaspoon black peppercorns

½ mace blade

¼ nutmeg, grated

1 teaspoon cumin seeds

1½ teaspoons coriander seeds

½ teaspoon fenugreek seeds

2 teaspoons garlic paste

1 tablespoon ginger paste

3 tablespoons apple cider vinegar or white wine vinegar

1 tablespoon tamarind juice or juice of ½ lime

1½ pound boneless leg of pork, cut into 1-inch cubes

¼ cup vegetable oil or peanut oil, plus 2 teaspoons

2 large onions, finely chopped

1¼ cups warm water

1 teaspoon salt, or to taste

1 teaspoon packed dark brown sugar

2 large garlic cloves, finely sliced

8–10 fresh curry leaves

1. Grind the first ten ingredients (all the spices) to a fine powder in a spice grinder. Transfer the ground spices to a bowl and add the garlic and ginger pastes, vinegar, and tamarind juice. Mix together to form a paste.

2. Put the pork into a large, nonmetallic bowl and rub about one-quarter of the spice paste into the meat. Cover and let marinate in the refrigerator for 30–40 minutes.

3. Heat the ¼ cup of oil in a heavy saucepan over medium heat, add the onions, and cook, stirring frequently, for 8–10 minutes, until lightly browned. Add the remaining spice paste and cook, stirring constantly, for 5–6 minutes. Add 2 tablespoons of the water and cook until it evaporates. Repeat with another 2 tablespoons of water.

4. Add the marinated pork and cook over medium-high heat for 5–6 minutes. Add the salt, sugar, and the remaining water. Bring to a boil, then reduce the heat to low, cover, and simmer for 50–55 minutes.

5. Meanwhile, heat the 2 teaspoons of oil in a small saucepan over low heat. Add the sliced garlic and cook, stirring, until it begins to brown. Add the curry leaves and let sizzle for 15–20 seconds. Stir the garlic mixture into the pan. Serve immediately.

RIB OF BEEF WITH A HOT HORSERADISH CRUST

| SERVES: 4–6 | PREP TIME: 10 mins | COOK TIME: 60 mins, plus resting |

A SPICY COATING OF CREAMED HORSERADISH AND MUSTARD MAKES THIS SUCCULENT RIB INTO SOMETHING EXTRA SPECIAL. CARVE IT FOR DINNER AND ANY LEFTOVERS WILL BE DELICIOUS SERVED COLD.

INGREDIENTS

4½ pounds rib of beef on the bone
1 teaspoon salt
1 teaspoon pepper
¼ cup olive oil

HORSERADISH CRUST

2 tablespoons extra virgin olive oil
¼ cup creamed horseradish
2 tablespoons English mustard
zest and juice of 1 lemon
½ teaspoon salt
½ teaspoon pepper

1. Preheat the oven to 350°F.

2. Place the rib of beef on a large cutting board and season with the salt and pepper.

3. Put all of the horseradish crust ingredients into a small bowl and mix until combined to a coarse paste.

4. Heat the olive oil in a large skillet over medium-high heat and seal the rib on all sides. Transfer to a wire rack positioned over a roasting pan and brush all over with the horseradish paste. Put the pan into the preheated oven and cook for 50 minutes.

5. Remove the rib from the oven and set aside to rest for about 30 minutes before serving. Serve with the juices from the roasting pan poured over the top.

COLOSSAL LAMB KABOB WITH HOT CHILI SAUCE

SERVES: 1	PREP TIME: 10 mins	COOK TIME: 10 mins

THESE SPICY HOT LAMB KABOBS ARE TRULY SIMPLE YET SERIOUSLY FILLING. PERFECT FOR THE BARBECUE OR FOR A SOLO EVENING MEAL, THE KABOB AND CHILI SAUCE CAN ALSO BE SERVED WITH HOT PITA BREAD.

INGREDIENTS

1 pound leg of lamb, diced
2 tablespoons olive oil
1 teaspoon dried thyme
1 teaspoon paprika
1 teaspoon ground cumin
1 large flatbread
1 small red onion, sliced
1 tomato, chopped
small bunch of fresh cilantro, chopped
½ lemon
salt and pepper
sriracha or other hot chili sauce and plain yogurt, to serve

1. In a medium bowl, mix the lamb with the olive oil, thyme, and spices and season with salt and pepper.

2. Preheat a large ridged grill pan or barbecue.

3. Thread the lamb onto two large metal skewers, and cook in the preheated pan for 4-5 minutes on each side, or until cooked to your liking.

4. Heat a large, dry skillet and cook the flatbread for a few seconds on both sides until soft.

5. Remove the lamb from the skewers, place on the flatbread, and top with the onion, tomato, and cilantro. Squeeze with the lemon and serve immediately with the sriracha and plain yogurt.

LAMB WITH
BLACK BEAN SAUCE

| SERVES: 4 | PREP TIME: 25 mins | COOK TIME: 12–14 mins |

FIVE-SPICE POWDER AND BLACK BEAN SAUCE CREATE SOME MAGIC WITH LAMB AND BELL PEPPERS TO GIVE THIS DISH PLENTY OF WARMTH AND PIZAZZ.

INGREDIENTS

1 pound boneless lamb shoulder or boneless lamb chops
1 egg white, lightly beaten
¼ cup cornstarch
1 teaspoon five-spice powder
3 tablespoons sunflower oil
1 red onion, sliced
1 red bell pepper, seeded and sliced
1 green bell pepper, seeded and sliced
1 yellow or orange bell pepper, seeded and sliced
⅓ cup black bean sauce
freshly cooked noodles, to serve

1. Using a sharp knife, slice the lamb into thin strips.

2. Mix together the egg white, cornstarch, and five-spice powder. Toss the lamb strips in the mixture until evenly coated.

3. Heat the oil in a preheated wok or large skillet and cook the lamb over high heat, stirring, for 5 minutes, or until it crisps around the edges.

4. Add the onion and bell pepper slices to the wok and stir-fry for 5–6 minutes, or until the vegetables just begin to soften.

5. Stir the black bean sauce into the lamb mixture in the wok and heat through.

6. Transfer the lamb and sauce to warm serving plates and serve hot with freshly cooked noodles.

TIP

BLACK BEAN SAUCE IS MADE WITH SALTY FERMENTED BEANS. CHECK THE FINISHED DISH FOR FLAVOR BEFORE ADDING ANY EXTRA SALT.

FISH & SEAFOOD MAINS

When you're in the mood for a taste of the sea, these zingy fish dishes will deliver a spicy punch of flavors to satisfy your cravings. Including shrimp, crayfish, scallops, and sardines, the succulent recipes feature Maharashtrian Salmon in a Sauce, Shrimp & Chile-Lime Spaghetti, Whole Spice-Crusted Red Snapper, and Crayfish Cakes with Mashed Avocado & Chile.

MAHARASHTRIAN
SALMON IN A SAUCE

SERVES: 4	PREP TIME: 5–10 mins	COOK TIME: 15–20 mins

THIS SIMPLE FISH DISH IS PACKED WITH FLAVOR. YOU CAN USE ANY FIRM FISH FILLET OR STEAKS INSTEAD OF THE SALMON, IF DESIRED. SERVE WITH FRESHLY COOKED RICE TO SOAK UP THE DELICIOUS COOKING LIQUID.

INGREDIENTS

⅓ cup vegetable or peanut oil

8 (5½-ounce) salmon steaks

2 teaspoons cornstarch

1 teaspoon hot chili powder

1 teaspoon paprika

½ teaspoon ground turmeric

2 teaspoons ground cumin

1 teaspoon ground coriander

2 teaspoons salt

1 teaspoon tamarind paste

1¾ cups coconut milk

1¾ cups cold water

1. Heat the oil in a nonstick saucepan and add the fish. Cook for 1–2 minutes on each side.

2. Mix together the cornstarch, spices, salt, tamarind paste, and coconut milk. Pour this mixture into the saucepan with the water.

3. Bring to a boil, then reduce the heat, cover, and cook gently for 10–12 minutes, or until the fish is cooked through and the sauce has thickened slightly (it should still be runny). Serve immediately.

SPICED BAKED COD
WITH HARISSA & PINE NUT CRUST
& ROAST CHERRY TOMATOES

SERVES: 2	PREP TIME: 10 mins	COOK TIME: 15 mins

THIS DISH IS INCREDIBLY QUICK TO PREPARE, AND MAKES A DELICIOUS, EASY MIDWEEK MEAL. THE SPICY, CRUNCHY TOPPING IS A WONDERFUL CONTRAST FOR THE SOFT FISH FLAKES.

INGREDIENTS

¼ cup pine nuts

⅓ cup fresh bread crumbs

grated zest of 1 unwaxed lemon

2 tablespoons coarsely chopped fresh cilantro

pinch of sea salt

1 teaspoon olive oil

20 cherry tomatoes (still on the vine)

2 (7-ounce) cod fillets

2 teaspoons rose harissa

1. Preheat the oven to 400°F. Crush the pine nuts in a mortar and pestle. Transfer them to a bowl, add the bread crumbs, lemon zest, cilantro, salt, and oil, and mix well.

2. Put the cherry tomatoes onto a large baking pan and add the cod fillets, skin side down, arranging everything in a single layer. Spread a teaspoon of rose harissa over each cod fillet, then top with the bread crumb mixture, pressing down gently.

3. Bake on a high shelf in the oven for 15 minutes, or until the topping is crisp and golden and the fish flakes easily when pressed with a knife. Serve the cod hot with the tomatoes.

TIP

SUBSTITUTE RED SNAPPER, HALIBUT, OR ANY OTHER FIRM WHITE FISH FOR THE COD—WHATEVER IS FRESHEST AND BEST VALUE ON THE DAY.

MOROCCAN FISH SOUP

SERVES: 4	PREP TIME: 20 mins	COOK TIME: 55 mins–1¼ hours

PREPARED WITH RED SNAPPER, THIS SOUP IS FULL OF RICH FLAVORS AND SPICY WARMTH PRODUCED BY THE RICH COMBINATION OF SPICES.

INGREDIENTS

2 tablespoons olive oil

1 large onion, finely chopped

pinch of saffron threads

½ teaspoon ground cinnamon

1 teaspoon ground coriander

½ teaspoon ground cumin

½ teaspoon ground turmeric

¾ cup canned diced tomatoes

1¼ cups fish broth or stock

4 small red snapper steaks

½ cup pitted green olives

1 tablespoon chopped preserved lemon

3 tablespoons chopped fresh cilantro

salt and pepper (optional)

couscous, to serve

1. Heat the oil in a flameproof casserole dish. Add the onion and cook over low heat, stirring occasionally, for 10 minutes, until soft, but not browned. Add the saffron, cinnamon, ground coriander, cumin, and turmeric and cook the mixture for an additional 30 seconds, stirring constantly.

2. Add the tomatoes and fish broth or stock and stir well. Bring to a boil, reduce the heat, cover, and simmer for 15 minutes. Uncover and simmer for 20–35 minutes, or until thickened.

3. Cut each red snapper in half, then add the fish pieces to the casserole, pushing them down into the liquid. Simmer the stew for an additional 5–6 minutes, or until the fish is just cooked.

4. Carefully stir in the olives, preserved lemon, and chopped cilantro. Season with salt and pepper, if using, and serve with couscous.

SHRIMP & CHILE-LIME SPAGHETTI

SERVES: 4	PREP TIME: 20–30 mins	COOK TIME: 30 mins

THIS DISH, COMBINING PLUMP, JUICY SHRIMP, ZUCCHINI, AND SPAGHETTI, WITH THE ADDED BITE OF JALAPEÑO CHILES, PROVIDES AN EASY MEAL.

INGREDIENTS

1–2 teaspoons salt
1 pound dried spaghetti
4 garlic cloves
2–4 red or green jalapeño chiles
4 small zucchini
3 scallions
2 tablespoons olive oil
1 pound peeled and deveined raw shrimp
finely grated zest and juice of 1 lime
2 tablespoons butter
salt (optional)

1. Add the salt to a large saucepan of water and bring to a boil, add the spaghetti, bring back to a boil, and cook for 8–10 minutes, or according to package directions, until tender but still firm to the bite. Meanwhile, peel and crush the garlic, seed and dice the chiles, dice the zucchini, and thinly slice the scallions.

2. Drain the pasta in a colander and set aside until needed. Return the pan to the heat, add the oil, and heat over medium-high heat. Add the garlic and cook, stirring, for 1–2 minutes, until it begins to soften. Add the chiles, zucchini ,and salt, if using, and cook, stirring occasionally, until the zucchini is beginning to brown.

3. Add the shrimp and lime juice and zest to the pan. Add the scallions and cook, stirring occasionally, until the shrimp are pink and cooked through. Add the butter and reserved spaghetti and cook, stirring, for 1–2 minutes, until most of the liquid has evaporated. Serve immediately.

DEEP-FRIED FISH WITH CHILI BEAN SAUCE

SERVES: 4–6	PREP TIME: 25 mins	COOK TIME: 20–25 mins

DEEP-FRIED FRESHWATER FISH WITH A TEMPTING SAUCE THAT COMBINES THE FLAVORS OF CHILE, GARLIC, GINGER, AND CHILI BEAN OFFERS UP A DIVINE TREAT WITH SOMETHING OF A KICK.

INGREDIENTS

4 whole freshwater fish, such as trout or carp (about 1 pound), gutted

1 tablespoon all-purpose flour

pinch of salt

⅓ cup water

vegetable oil or peanut oil, for deep-frying

SAUCE

⅓ cup vegetable oil or peanut oil

1 teaspoon crushed red pepper flakes

1 garlic clove, finely chopped

1 teaspoon finely chopped fresh ginger

1 tablespoon chili bean sauce

½ teaspoon white pepper

2 teaspoons sugar

1 tablespoon white rice vinegar

1 teaspoon finely chopped scallion

1. To prepare the fish, clean and dry thoroughly. Mix together the flour, salt, and water to create a light batter. Coat the fish.

2. Heat enough oil for deep-frying in a wok, deep fryer, or large heavy saucepan to 350–375°F, or until a cube of bread browns in 30 seconds. Deep-fry the fish until the skin is crisp and golden brown. Drain, set aside, and keep warm.

3. To make the sauce, first heat all but 1 tablespoon of the oil in a small saucepan and, when smoking, pour in the red pepper flakes. Set aside.

4. In a preheated wok or deep saucepan, heat the remaining oil and stir-fry the garlic and ginger until fragrant. Stir in the chili bean sauce, then add the oil-red pepper flake mixture. Season with the pepper, sugar, and vinegar. Turn off the heat and stir in the scallion. Pour over the fish and serve immediately.

FISH IN TOMATO & CHILI SAUCE WITH FRIED ONIONS

SERVES: 4	PREP TIME: 10 mins, plus marinating	COOK TIME: 35–40 mins

FIRM-FLESHED FISH IS PAN-FRIED UNTIL BROWNED AND THEN SIMMERED IN AN ALLURINGLY SPICED CHILI-AND-TOMATO SAUCE. THIS DISH IS BEST SERVED WITH FRESHLY COOKED RICE AND POPPADOMS.

INGREDIENTS

1½ pounds white fish fillets, such as halibut, cod, or red snapper, cut into 5-cm/ 2-inch pieces

2 tablespoons lemon juice

1 teaspoon salt, or to taste

1 teaspoon ground turmeric

¼ cup vegetable oil or peanut oil, plus extra for pan-frying

2 teaspoons sugar

1 large onion, finely chopped

2 teaspoons ginger paste

2 teaspoons garlic paste

½ teaspoon ground fennel seeds

1 teaspoon ground coriander

½–1 teaspoon chili powder

⅔ cup canned diced tomatoes

1¼ cups warm water

2–3 tablespoons chopped fresh cilantro

1. Place the fish on a large plate and gently rub in the lemon juice, ½ teaspoon of the salt, and ½ teaspoon of the turmeric. Set aside for 15–20 minutes.

2. Pour enough oil into a skillet to fill to a depth of about ½ inch and place over medium–high heat. When the oil is hot, cook the pieces of fish, in a single layer, until well browned on both sides and a light crust is formed. Drain on paper towels.

3. Heat the ¼ cup of oil in a saucepan or skillet over medium heat and add the sugar. Let it brown, watching it carefully because once it browns, it will blacken quickly. As soon as the sugar is brown, add the onion and cook for 5 minutes, until soft. Add the ginger and garlic pastes and cook for an additional 3–4 minutes, or until the mixture begins to brown.

4. Add the ground fennel seeds, ground coriander, chili powder, and the remaining turmeric. Cook for about a minute, then add half the tomatoes. Stir and cook until the tomato juice has evaporated, then add the remaining tomatoes. Continue to cook, stirring, until the oil separates from the spice paste.

5. Pour in the water and add the remaining salt. Bring to a boil and reduce the heat to medium. Add the fish, stir gently ,and reduce the heat to low. Cook, uncovered, for 5–6 minutes, then stir in half the chopped cilantro and remove from the heat. Garnish with the remaining cilantro and serve immediately.

GROW YOUR OWN CHILES

We know you love the taste of chiles . . . but did you realize they're easy to grow yourself? It is not necessary to live in a hot country or near the equator—with some care, anyone can nurture a crop.

The good news for aspiring chile growers is that you don't need a yard—chiles grow best in flowerpots, so just a little amount of outdoor space is enough, even a hanging basket, or inside on a windowsill.

1. Sow seeds indoors six to eight weeks before the last expected frost. Wait until nighttime temperature stays above 55°F before moving the plants outdoors.

2. Fill a seed module flat with seed-starting mix, lightly water, and place a seed in each cell or compartment of the tray. Put some more seed-starting mix on top. Water again, cover with plastic wrap, and put somewhere warm. Check them every day and keep the plants moist.

3. After a month you should see sprouts coming through (see opposite, above left). Remove the plastic wrap and move to a warm windowsill. Keep moist.

4. When your seedlings sprout a second set of leaves, carefully transplant to small flowerpots, and encourage growth with a weekly tomato fertilizer.

5. At about 5 inches tall, transplant to bigger flowerpots. Support any drooping plants by tying them to a stake, important because their roots are shallow. In hot weather, plant outdoors in full sun in a soil enriched with organic matter that is moisture retentive and drains well.

6. Try not to let your plants grow above 12 inches tall—if you pinch the tops above the leaves, you will encourage bushiness and more flowers.

7. As the plants develop, flowers will start to appear on your plants.

8. Start giving the plants a liquid fertilizer once the flowers appear, or just before they start to form, and carry on until the chiles has been harvested. Fertilize the plants every two weeks.

9. After flowering, the flowers will turn brown and drop off. This is normal and indicates that a chile is pushing its way through the flower. Keep the plant fertilized and watered as the chiles ripen.

10. Harvest your chile peppers by removing them from plants with a sharp knife or pruners to prevent any damage to the plant. Snip off (and eat) the first crop while they're still green—this will encourage additional chiles to form.

TOP TIPS

Water chile plants regularly, especially in hot weather. Chile plants thrive in the light, so give them plenty to be sure of a fast, strong growth.

Pick chiles regularly to make sure that the plant directs its resources toward producing more of them.

The best color and flavor will come from chiles that are allowed to ripen to a good color, but be aware that leaving chiles on the plant will suppress the production of new ones.

Fresh hot chiles will keep in the refrigerator for one week or in a cool, dry position for up to two weeks.

MONKFISH & BABY BROCCOLI
COCONUT SOUP

SERVES: 4	PREP TIME: 15 mins	COOK TIME: 20 mins

FISH, COCONUT, AND SPICES WERE SIMPLY MADE FOR EACH OTHER, AS YOU'LL KNOW IF YOU TRY THIS QUICK-AND-SIMPLE SOUP FOR DINNER.

INGREDIENTS

1 large onion, chopped

2 teaspoon Thai fish sauce

juice of ½ lime

1 red chile, stem removed

1 green chile, stem removed

2 teaspoons crushed coriander seeds

2 teaspoons crushed cumin seeds

1-inch piece fresh ginger, chopped

3 garlic cloves, coarsely chopped

½ lemongrass stalk

1½ tablespoons peanut oil

5 curry leaves

1¼ cups coconut milk

12 ounces baby broccoli, each spear cut into two pieces

1 pound monkfish fillet, cubed

1 red chile, sliced

1. Add the onion, fish sauce, lime juice, chiles, seeds, ginger, garlic, lemongrass, and half of the oil to the bowl of a blender or food processor and process until you have a paste. Pour the mixture into a skillet and cook over medium heat for 2 minutes. Stir in the curry leaves and coconut milk and simmer for an additional 10 minutes.

2. Meanwhile, add the remaining oil to another skillet and put over high heat. Stir-fry the baby broccoli for 2 minutes, or until just tender. Set aside.

3. Add the monkfish cubes to the pan with the spices and bring back to a simmer. Cook for 2 minutes, then add the broccoli spears to the pan and continue cooking for an additional minute. Serve the soup with the sliced chile sprinkled over the top.

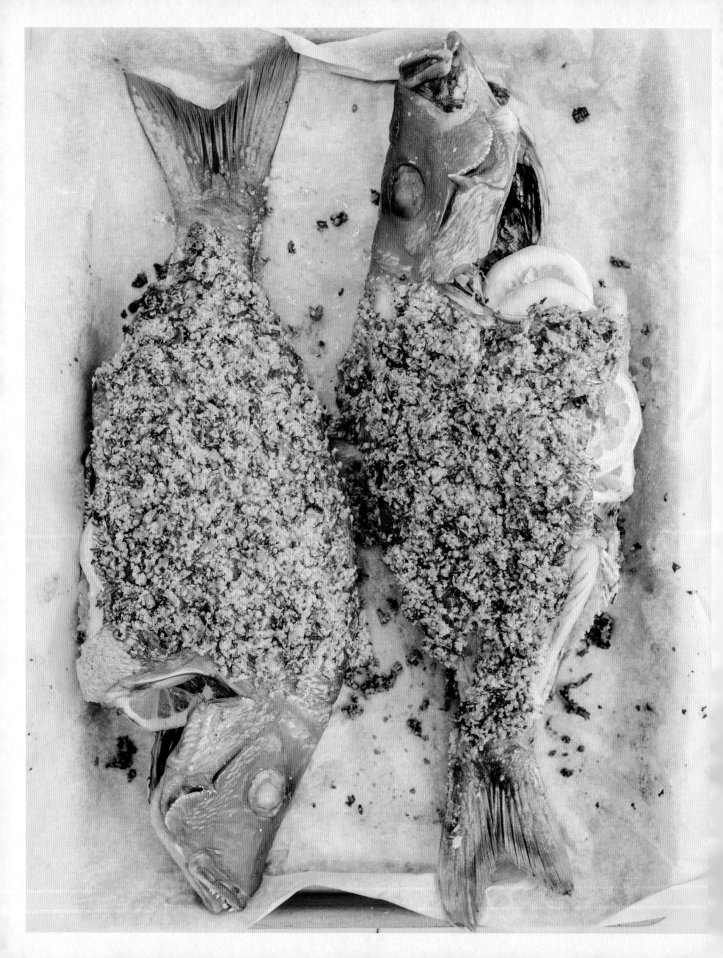

WHOLE SPICE-CRUSTED
RED SNAPPER

SERVES: 2	PREP TIME: 10 mins	COOK TIME: 20 mins

THE SPICES HERE HAVE JUST THE RIGHT AMOUNT OF HEAT AND FLAVOR TO COMPLEMENT THE FISH AND GIVE IT A CRISP CRUST THAT CONTRASTS WITH ITS SOFT FLESH. THE RECIPE IS EASILY SCALED UP IF YOU'RE COOKING FOR MORE THAN TWO PEOPLE. SERVE WITH STEAMED VEGETABLES OR SEA BEANS (ASPARAGUS).

INGREDIENTS

2 whole red snappers, scaled and gutted

1 lemon, thinly sliced

3½ teaspoons dukkah spice

⅔ cup ground almonds (almond meal)

¼ cup olive oil

¼ cup finely chopped fresh cilantro

2 teaspoons sea salt flakes

grated zest of 1 unwaxed lemon

1. Preheat the oven to 400°F. Line a large roasting pan with parchment paper and lay the fish on top.

2. Mix the lemon zest, dukkah spice, ground almonds, oil, cilantro, and salt together in a bowl.

3. Spoon 2 tablespoons of the mixture over one side of each fish, pressing it down gently to make a crust. Turn each fish over and spoon 2 tablespoons of the mixture on the other side. Put any remaining mixture in the cavities. Divide the lemon slices between the cavities.

4. Roast for 20 minutes, or until the fish flakes easily when tested with a knife. Let rest for 2 minutes before serving hot.

TIP

WHEN BUYING WHOLE FISH, LOOK FOR BRIGHT AND CLEAR EYES, SHINY SKIN, AND BRIGHT-RED GILLS, AND MAKE SURE IT SMELLS FRESH.

CRAYFISH CAKES
WITH MASHED AVOCADO & CHILE

SERVES: 4	PREP TIME: 15 mins, plus chilling	COOK TIME: 5–10 mins

TASTY CRAYFISH TAILS ARE A DELIGHTFULLY LOW-FAT TREAT AND, ALTHOUGH THEY DO CONTAIN CHOLESTEROL, THEY CAN BE ENJOYED AS PART OF A BALANCED, HEART-FRIENDLY DIET.

INGREDIENTS

²⁄₃ cup fresh whole-wheat bread crumbs

½ teaspoon pepper

2 tablespoons finely chopped fresh flat-leaf parsley

8 ounces peeled and cooked crayfish tails, coarsely chopped

¼ cup drained, chopped roasted red bell pepper from a jar

1 teaspoon medium-hot peri peri sauce

1 tablespoon extra-light mayonnaise

1 medium egg white, beaten

1 tablespoon flour, for dusting

6 sprays cooking oil spray

MASHED AVOCADO & CHILE

1 ripe avocado, peeled, pitted, and sliced

1 small fresh red chile, seeded and finely chopped

1 scallion, finely chopped

½ teaspoon smoked paprika

juice of ¼ lime

1. Put the bread crumbs, pepper, and parsley into a bowl and stir well to combine.

2. In a separate bowl, combine the crayfish tails, red bell pepper, peri peri sauce, and mayonnaise. Stir the bread crumb mixture into the crayfish mixture.

3. Add the beaten egg white and mix to a moderately firm mixture; the cakes will be firm once they are cooked. Divide and shape into four round cakes and sprinkle with flour. If you have time, chill for up to 1 hour.

4. To make the mashed avocado, put the avocado slices into a bowl and coarsely mash with a fork. Stir in the chile, scallion, paprika, and lime juice.

5. Spray a nonstick skillet with the cooking oil spray and put over medium-high heat. Add the crayfish cakes and cook for 2–3 minutes, or until the underside is crisp and golden. Turn and cook for an additional 2–3 minutes, or until cooked through. Serve the cakes immediately with the mashed avocado on the side.

FISH WITH CHILE, WHITE WINE & TAPENADE

SERVES: 4	PREP TIME: 5 mins	COOK TIME: 15 mins

THIS FISH, CHILE, AND TAPENADE DISH IS A BREEZE TO PREPARE, AND YET IT ALSO DELIVERS SOME SOPHISTICATED FLAVORS.

INGREDIENTS

1 tablespoon olive oil

4 white fish fillets

¼ cup tapenade

1 small red finger chile, seeded and chopped

¼ cup freshly grated Parmesan cheese

¼ cup dry white wine

salt and pepper (optional)

3½ cups cooked rice, to serve

1. Preheat the oven to 425°F. Brush a wide, ovenproof dish with the oil.

2. Season the fish with salt and pepper, if using, and place in the prepared dish in a single layer.

3. Mix the tapenade and chile together and spread over the fish, then sprinkle with the cheese.

4. Pour the wine around the fish and bake in the preheated oven for about 15 minutes, or until the flesh flakes easily. Serve with the rice.

SEARED SCALLOPS
WITH FRESH MINT
& RED CHILE DRESSING

SERVES: 4–6	PREP TIME: 35 mins	COOK TIME: 25–28 mins

ENJOY THESE SEARED SCALLOPS ON A BED OF PEPPERY GREENS, WITH HERBED LENTILS, PAN-FRIED PANCETTA, AND A DRIZZLE OF MINT-CHILE DRESSING.

INGREDIENTS

½ cup French green lentils

2 garlic cloves

1 celery stalk

2 bay leaves

20 fresh parsley leaves, with stems

olive oil, for drizzling and frying

zest and juice of 1 lemon

2 tablespoons aged red wine vinegar

20 fresh basil leaves,
coarsely chopped

20 fresh mint leaves,
coarsely chopped

handful of arugula leaves,
coarsely chopped

20 scallops

8 slices pancetta

salt and pepper (optional)

peppery salad greens, to serve

MINT & RED CHILE DRESSING

2 red chiles, seeded and chopped

small bunch of fresh mint,
finely chopped

½ cup extra virgin olive oil

juice of 1 lemon

salt and pepper (optional)

1. Cover the lentils with water in a large saucepan and add the garlic, celery stalk, bay leaves, and a few parsley stems. Bring to a boil, then reduce to a simmer.

2. Cook the lentils for 12–15 minutes, until they are al dente and nutty. Remove from the heat and drain off most of the water. Remove the garlic, bay leaves, celery stalk, and parsley stems. Season the lentils with olive oil, lemon zest and juice, some of the vinegar, and salt and pepper, if using.

3. When the lentils have cooled slightly, add the herbs and arugula and stir until combined. Set the lentils aside.

4. For the dressing, mix together the chiles and mint in a bowl with the olive oil and the lemon juice, and season with salt and pepper, if using.

5. Clean the scallops by removing the small opaque muscle from the sides, and dry them on paper towels. Add a tablespoon of oil to a skillet over high heat, add the pancetta and cook the slices for 2 minutes on each side, until crispy. Drain on paper towels.

6. Keep the skillet over high heat. Pat the scallops until dry. Add a splash more olive oil to the skillet. Add the scallops and cook for 45 seconds. To turn the scallops, quickly use two tablespoons, one in each hand. Flick the scallops over from one spoon to the other. Cook on the second side for about 40 seconds; when the scallops are caramelized on both sides, remove and place on clean paper towels.

7. Add a splash of vinegar to deglaze the skillet, then add the liquid to the dressing. To serve, sprinkle the herbed lentils over the salad greens, and arrange the scallops and the pancetta on top. Spoon some mint and chile dressing on top and serve immediately.

BAKED FISH
WRAPPED IN BANANA LEAVES

SERVES: 4	PREP TIME: 15–20 mins	COOK TIME: 15–20 mins

THIS DELICIOUS INDIAN BAKED FISH DISH LOOKS PRETTY SERVED WRAPPED UP IN BANANA LEAVES. YOUR GUESTS WILL ENJOY THE MOUTHWATERING AROMAS THAT ARE RELEASED AS THEY UNWRAP THEIR INDIVIDUAL PACKAGES AT THE TABLE.

INGREDIENTS

4 (7-ounce) thick cod fillets, skinned
2 teaspoons ground turmeric
1 large fresh banana leaf

SPICE PASTE

2 teaspoons ground cumin
2 teaspoons ground coriander
1½ teaspoons palm sugar or brown sugar
1 cup coconut cream
4 fresh red chiles, seeded and chopped
2½ cups chopped fresh cilantro
¼ cup chopped fresh mint
5 garlic cloves, chopped
1 teaspoon finely grated fresh ginger
¼ cup vegetable oil or peanut oil
juice of 2 limes
2 teaspoon salt

1. Preheat the oven to 400°F.

2. Place the fish fillets in a single layer on a plate and sprinkle with the turmeric. Rub into the fish and set aside.

3. Put the ingredients for the spice paste into a food processor and blend until fairly smooth.

4. Cut the banana leaf into four 9½-inch squares. Soften the banana leaf squares by dipping them into a saucepan of hot water for a few seconds. Once the banana leaf squares have become pliant, wipe them dry with paper towels and arrange on a work surface.

5. Apply the spice paste liberally to both sides of each piece of fish. Place a piece of fish on top of each banana leaf square and wrap up like a package, securing with bamboo skewers or twine.

6. Place the packages on a baking pan and bake in the preheated oven for 15–20 minutes, until cooked through. Transfer to plates and serve immediately.

BAKING, DESSERTS & DRINKS

Sweet and spicy flavors can complement each other
surprisingly well, as you'll discover with this irresistible
selection of spice-infused cakes, desserts, and drinks.
Go ahead and indulge in smooth Chocolate Mousse
with a Chile Kick; Spicy Squash Cake; Carrot, Fruit
& Cardamom Rolls; or blast your socks off with
a Chile & Wasabi Bloody Mary.

CHOCOLATE MOUSSE WITH A CHILE KICK

SERVES: 4	PREP TIME: 20 mins, plus chilling	COOK TIME: 5 mins

CHOCOLATE AND CHILE MIGHT NOT FEEL LIKE A NATURAL PAIRING, BUT THEY WORK TOGETHER WONDERFULLY—A SUBTLE NOTE OF CHILE BRINGS A DELIGHTFUL WARMTH TO THIS SMOOTH CHOCOLATE MOUSSE.

INGREDIENTS

6 ounces bittersweet chocolate, broken into pieces

pinch of salt

4 extra-large eggs, separated

¼ cup superfine sugar

⅔ cup heavy cream

1 teaspoon chipotle powder

2 teaspoons orange zest

⅔ cup sour cherries

½ cup dark rum

½ cup roasted hazelnuts

1. Put the chocolate pieces into a large heatproof bowl set over a saucepan of gently simmering water and heat, stirring occasionally, until melted. Remove from the heat and set aside to cool.

2. Once the chocolate has cooled, beat in the salt, egg yolks, and sugar.

3. In a separate bowl whisk the heavy cream until it thickens slightly.

4. In a clean bowl whisk the egg whites until stiff peaks form.

5. Add the chipotle powder and 1 teaspoon of the orange zest to the chocolate mixture, then fold in the cream, followed by the egg whites. Divide among four glasses and place in the refrigerator for 2 hours to set.

6. Meanwhile, soak the sour cherries in the rum and coarsely chop the hazelnuts.

7. Just before serving remove the mousse from the refrigerator and top with the rum-soaked sour cherries, the hazelnuts, and the remaining orange zest.

CINNAMON-SPICED
SYLLABUB

SERVES: 8	PREP TIME: 10 mins, plus chilling	COOK TIME: none

WONDERFULLY EASY TO MAKE, THESE LITTLE CLOUDS OF LIGHTLY WHIPPED CREAM WILL LOOK BEAUTIFUL PILED INTO YOUR PRETTIEST GLASSES. YOUR GUESTS WILL LOVE THEIR MIDDLE-EASTERN SCENT OF CINNAMON AND ORANGE FLOWER WATER.

INGREDIENTS

juice of 2 lemons

½ teaspoon ground cinnamon, plus a pinch to decorate

1 teaspoon orange flower water

½ cup superfine sugar

2½ cups heavy cream

1 tablespoon chopped pistachio nuts, to decorate

2 tablespoons pomegranate seeds, to decorate

1. Put the lemon juice, cinnamon, orange flower water, and sugar into a large bowl and whisk briefly to dissolve the sugar. Add the cream and lightly whisk until it just comes together as barely solid—this should take no more than 1 minute.

2. Spoon the syllabub into eight small ½-cup glasses. Sprinkle with the remaining cinnamon, the pistachio nuts, and pomegranate seeds. Cover and chill in the refrigerator for at least 1 hour, or up to a day. Serve cold.

TIP

SYLLABUB SHOULD NOT BE THE TEXTURE OF WHIPPED CREAM, SO BE CAREFUL NOT TO OVERWHISK IT AFTER ADDING THE CREAM.

APRICOTS POACHED IN ROSEWATER & CARDAMOM WITH GINGER YOGURT

SERVES: 4	PREP TIME: 20 mins	COOK TIME: 15 mins

THIS IS ONE OF THE EASIEST DESSERTS TO MAKE, AND THE APRICOTS WILL BRING SOME SUNSHINE TO THE TABLE. YOUR GUESTS WILL BE DELIGHTED BY ITS EXOTIC FRAGRANCE AND GENTLY SPICED FLAVOR.

INGREDIENTS

¼ cup superfine sugar

6 green cardamom pods, lightly crushed

1 cinnamon stick

¼ teaspoon rosewater

1½ cups water

4 apricots, halved and pitted

1 tablespoon dried edible rose petals, to decorate (optional)

GINGER YOGURT

½ cup Greek-style plain yogurt

1-inch piece of fresh ginger, peeled and finely grated

1. Put the sugar, cardamom, cinnamon, rosewater, and water into a saucepan, stir and cook over low heat until the sugar has dissolved.

2. Increase the heat to medium–high, bring to a boil, then lower in the apricots, using a slotted spoon. Reduce the heat to low and simmer for 5 minutes. Turn off the heat and let them stand in the syrup for 10 minutes.

3. Transfer the apricots to a serving bowl, using the slotted spoon. When cool enough to handle, slip off and discard the skins.

4. For the ginger yogurt, put the yogurt in a small serving bowl, stir in the ginger, cover, and set aside.

5. Return the syrup to the heat and boil until reduced by half. Pour the syrup over the apricots, then sprinkle with the dried rose petals, if using. Serve the apricots with the ginger yogurt. If not serving immediately, let cool, then cover and chill in the refrigerator and serve cold.

TIP

ROSEWATER COMES IN DIFFERENT STRENGTHS, DEPENDING ON THE MAKE. ADJUST ACCORDING TO YOUR BRAND AND TASTE.

INDIAN
RICE DESSERT

SERVES: 4 | **PREP TIME**: 20–25 mins, plus soaking and chilling | **COOK TIME**: 30–35 mins

FOR THIS DISH, RICE FLOUR IS COOKED IN THICKENED MILK WITH APRICOTS, RAISINS, ALMONDS, AND PISTACHIO NUTS, WITH THE EXOTIC AROMA OF ROSEWATER AND CARDAMOM. IT IS BEST SERVED CHILLED.

INGREDIENTS

good pinch of saffron threads, pounded
2 tablespoons hot milk
3 tablespoons clarified butter or unsalted butter
⅓ cup rice flour
¼ cup slivered almonds
3 tablespoons seedless raisins
2½ cups whole milk
2 cups evaporated milk
¼ cup superfine sugar
12 dried apricots, sliced
1 teaspoon freshly ground cardamom seeds
½ teaspoon freshly grated nutmeg
2 tablespoons rosewater

TO DECORATE
¼ cup walnut pieces
2 tablespoons shelled unsalted pistachio nuts

1. Put the pounded saffron into the hot milk and soak until needed.

2. Reserve 2 teaspoons of the butter and melt the remainder in a heavy saucepan over low heat. Add the rice flour, almonds, and raisins and cook, stirring, for 2 minutes. Add the whole milk, increase the heat to medium, and cook, stirring, until it begins to bubble gently. Reduce the heat to low and cook, stirring frequently, for 10–12 minutes, to prevent the mixture from sticking to the bottom of the pan.

3. Add the evaporated milk, sugar, and apricots, reserving a few slices to decorate. Cook, stirring, until the mixture thickens but can still be poured.

4. Add the cardamom, nutmeg ,and rosewater, stir to distribute well, and remove from the heat. Let cool, then cover and chill in the refrigerator for at least 2 hours.

5. Melt the reserved butter in a small saucepan over low heat. Add the walnuts and cook, stirring, until they brown a little. Remove and drain on paper towels. Brown the pistachio nuts in the remaining butter in the saucepan, remove, and drain on paper towels. Let the pistachio nuts cool, then lightly crush.

6. Serve the dessert decorated with the fried nuts and the reserved apricot slices.

CHILE & CHOCOLATE CHURROS

| MAKES: 16 | PREP TIME: 35 mins, plus cooling | COOK TIME: 30–35 mins |

CHURROS ARE FRIED-DOUGH PASTRY SNACKS—IN THIS YUMMY VERSION, SEMISWEET CHOCOLATE, COCOA, CHILE, AND CREAM DO THEM PROUD.

INGREDIENTS

1 stick unsalted butter, diced
1 cup water
1¼ cups all-purpose flour, sifted
large pinch of salt
2 extra-large eggs, beaten
½ small red chile, seeded and minced
oil, for deep-frying
¼ cup sugar
2 teaspoons unsweetened cocoa powder, sifted

CHOCOLATE SAUCE

3 ounces semisweet chocolate, broken into pieces
½ cup heavy cream
½ teaspoon vanilla extract
1 teaspoon crushed red pepper flakes

1. To make the chocolate sauce, put the chocolate and cream into a heatproof bowl set over a saucepan of gently simmering water and heat until the chocolate is melted. Remove from the heat and stir until smooth, then stir in the vanilla extract and red pepper flakes. Set aside and keep warm.

2. Put the butter and water into a large saucepan over low heat and heat until the butter has melted. Bring to a boil, remove from the heat, and add the flour and salt. Beat thoroughly until the mixture is smooth and comes away from the side of the pan. Let cool for 5 minutes, then gradually beat in the eggs to make a thick and glossy paste. Beat in the chile.

3. Heat enough oil for deep-frying in a large saucepan or deep fryer to 350–375°F, or until a cube of bread browns in 30 seconds. Spoon the paste into a large pastry bag fitted with a large star tip and pipe four 4-inch lengths of the paste into the hot oil. Fry for 2–3 minutes, turning frequently, until crisp and golden. Remove with a slotted spoon and drain on paper towels. Keep warm while frying the remaining mixture.

4. Mix together the sugar and cocoa powder on a flat plate and toss the warm churros in the mixture to coat. Serve immediately with the chocolate sauce for dipping.

SPICES FROM BARKS, FLOWER BUDS & ROOTS

Spices can be sourced from arils, barks, dried flower buds, stigmas, and roots, or from dried fruits or seeds. Here are a selection falling into the first category, as well as some mixed-spice combinations.

Cinnamon (see opposite, above left) is obtained from the inner bark of the *Cinnamomum* tree, which is native to Sri Lanka. The bark is dried and rolled up to make the long, slender tubes that characterize this spice. Cinnamon is also sold as a powder. Cinnamon is used in both savory and sweet dishes.

Cloves (see opposite, bottom right) are the aromatic dried red flower buds of *Syzygium aromaticum*, an evergreen tree from eastern Indonesia. They have a hard surround and contain an oily compound that creates the distinctive warm, sweet, aromatic taste. Cloves are used to give aromatic qualities to hot drinks and are often used in spice blends.

Coriander, known as cilantro in its leaf form, is used for its leaves and seeds. The leaves have a subtle citrus quality whereas the dried coriander seeds, of which there are two in each fruit, have a much stronger lemony flavor and bring warm, spicy overtones. Ground coriander is used as a key feature of various spice mixtures, such as garam masala and harissa.

Curry powder is a premixed combination of spices, usually chili powder, turmeric, coriander, cumin, ginger, and pepper. Strengths can vary from mild to strong. It it believed to have been created by the British to re-create the depth of flavor in Indian spice dishes, although spice mixtures are also common throughout Asia.

Ginger is a hot, fragrant spice obtained from the rhizome of the ginger plant *Zingiber officinale,* and the bulbous roots are widely used in southern Asian cuisines for beverages, soups, sauces, and baking. It is available fresh or ground and can be used in sweet and savory dishes.

Mace is obtained from the aril of the nutmeg plant, *Myristica fragrans*—the aril is the dried reddish covering of the nutmeg seed. The flavor, although similar to nutmeg, is lighter and sweeter and it has a more intense aroma.

Saffron is a spice from the flower stigma of the saffron crocus, *Crocus sativus* (see opposite, above right), which is native to southwest Asia. The flowers each have three vivid crimson stigmas, and it is from these that the threads are collected and dried. It is available in bright-red threads, which carry a musty, floral aroma and flavor. Labor-intensive to produce, saffron is one of the more expensive spices.

Turmeric (see opposite, bottom left) comes from the root of *Curcuma longa* and has a peppery, bitter flavor with orange and ginger overtones. It is used in mustard, which gives it its bright-yellow shade.

Za'atar is the name of a herb, but also of a spice mixture made from a combination of dried herbs, spices, and seeds, such as sesame seeds, dried sumac, and salt. Za'atar is widely used in Middle Eastern cooking.

SPICY SQUASH CAKE

| SERVES: 8 | PREP TIME: 35–40 mins, plus soaking | COOK TIME: 1¼ hrs |

BUTTERNUT SQUASH ADDS A RICH TEXTURE AND DEPTH TO SWEET CAKES AND MAKES A WONDERFUL COMPLEMENT TO DRIED FRUIT AND WARMING SPICES.

INGREDIENTS

⅓ cup golden raisins

2 teaspoons unsalted butter, for greasing

2 cups peeled, seeded, and diced butternut squash

1¼ sticks plus 1 tablespoon unsalted butter

¾ cup superfine or granulated sugar

½ cup chopped almonds

¼ cup Italian candied peel

finely grated zest of 1 lemon

1½ teaspoons ground cinnamon

1½ teaspoons ground ginger

¾ cup Kamut flour

1 heaping teaspoon baking powder

2 eggs, separated

1 tablespoons confectioners' sugar, for dusting

1. Put the golden raisins into a bowl, pour over enough boiling water to cover, and let soak.

2. Preheat the oven to 350°F. Grease and line a 9-inch round springform cake pan.

3. Put the squash and butter into a saucepan. Cover and cook over medium heat for about 15 minutes, until soft. Transfer to a bowl and beat until smooth.

4. Stir in the sugar, almonds, candied peel, lemon zest, cinnamon, ginger, and drained golden raisins, and mix well to combine.

5. Sift together the flour and baking powder, tipping in any bran remaining in the sifter. Gradually beat into the squash mixture.

6. Beat the egg yolks for about 3 minutes, until thick. Fold into the squash mixture.

7. Whisk the egg whites until they hold stiff peaks. Fold carefully into the mixture using a large metal spoon. Spoon the batter into the prepared pan.

8. Bake in the preheated oven for 1 hour, or until a toothpick inserted into the center comes out clean. Turn out onto a wire rack to cool. Dust with the confectioners' sugar just before serving.

CARROT, FRUIT
& CARDAMOM ROLLS

| MAKES: 16 | PREP TIME: 50–55 mins, plus standing/rising | COOK TIME: 30–35 mins |

THE CARROT TAKES CENTER STAGE IN THESE DELICIOUS SCANDINAVIAN-STYLE ROLLS. BURSTING WITH CANDIED FRUIT AND LIGHTLY SPICED WITH CARDAMOM, THEY ARE HEAVENLY WHEN EATEN FRESHLY BAKED.

INGREDIENTS

1 cup sliced carrots

2¾ cups white bread flour, sifted

2 tablespoons active dry yeast

3 tablespoons superfine sugar

2 teaspoons ground cardamom seeds (from about 24 pods)

½ teaspoon salt

1 stick unsalted butter

1 egg, lightly beaten

⅓ cup lukewarm milk

1 tablespoon flour, for dusting

1 tablespoon oil, for oiling

⅔ cup chopped candied fruit

1 egg yolk

1 tablespoon cold milk

1 tablespoon confectioners' sugar, for sprinkling

1. Put the carrots into the top of a steamer and steam for 15 minutes, until tender, then blend to a paste in a blender. Set aside until needed.

2. Line a baking pan with a silicone sheet. Put the flour, yeast, superfine sugar, cardamom, and salt into a large bowl and mix to combine. Melt all but 2 tablespoons of the butter and let cool slightly. Mix the beaten egg with the lukewarm milk and the melted butter. Stir into the flour mixture, then add the carrot paste. Mix to a soft dough.

3. Turn out the dough onto a floured board and knead for 10–15 minutes, until silky. Transfer to a lightly oiled bowl, cover with plastic wrap, and let stand in a warm place for 1½–2 hours, or until doubled in size. Turn out onto a floured board and punch down to get rid of the air. Roll out thinly to a 17½ x 12-inch rectangle.

4. Melt the remaining butter and brush it over the dough surface. Sprinkle with the candied fruit, taking it to the edge of the dough and breaking up any clumps.

5. Roll up the dough from the long edge into a log. Slice into 1-inch circles and place on the prepared baking pan. Cover with plastic wrap and let stand for 30 minutes. Meanwhile, preheat the oven to 400°F.

6. Mix the egg yolk with the cold milk and brush over the rolls, then bake in the preheated oven for 10–15 minutes, until golden.

7. Transfer to a wire rack to cool, then sprinkle with the confectioners' sugar. The rolls are best eaten freshly baked.

CHOCOLATE
PECAN BROWNIES WITH CHILE

MAKES: 12	PREP TIME: 30 mins	COOK TIME: 20–25 mins

HOW ABOUT SOME GORGEOUSLY STICKY, CHEWY BROWNIES WITH A DIFFERENCE? THE CHILE FLAVORING IN THESE IS SUBTLE ENOUGH TO WAKE UP THE TASTE BUDS WITHOUT SHOCKING THE PALATE.

INGREDIENTS

3½ tablespoons unsalted butter, softened, plus extra for greasing

½ cup granulated sugar

3 eggs, beaten

¾ cup all-purpose flour

¾ teaspoon baking powder

1 cup unsweetened cocoa powder

1 teaspoon crushed red pepper flakes

about 1 tablespoon rum

1 cup pecan halves

1. Preheat the oven to 350°F. Grease an 8-inch square or equivalent-size rectangular shallow baking pan.

2. Using a wooden spoon, beat the butter with sugar in a warm bowl until pale and fluffy. Alternatively, process in a food processor. Beat in the eggs, a little at a time, adding a little flour if the mixture begins to curdle. Switching to a metal spoon, gently fold in the flour, baking powder, cocoa powder, and red pepper flakes. Stir in the rum and add enough water until you have a cake batter that drops easily from the spoon. Taste and see if you need to add a little more chile. Fold in the pecans, reserving a few of the best for the top.

3. Pour the batter into the prepared pan, smoothing it into the corners. Sprinkle the top with the reserved pecan.

4. Bake in the preheated oven for 20–25 minutes, or until crusted on top but still not quite set. Remove from the oven and cut into 12 squares while still warm.

SPICED PUMPKIN
TARTS

| SERVES: 4 | PREP TIME: 30 mins, plus cooling | COOK TIME: 40 mins |

THESE GREAT INDIVIDUAL MINI TARTS HAVE ALL THE FLAVOR OF TRADITIONAL PUMPKIN PIE. THEY'RE SIMPLY DELICIOUS SERVED WITH COFFEE, OR AS AN INDULGENT DESSERT, WITH A LOT OF WHIPPED CREAM OR VANILLA ICE CREAM.

INGREDIENTS

2 teaspoons butter, for greasing

3½ cups (½-inch) pumpkin or butternut squash pieces

2 teaspoons butter

1 tablespoon maple syrup

1 piece preserved ginger in syrup, finely chopped

¼ teaspoon cinnamon

¼ teaspoon allspice

6 sheets of phyllo pastry

2 tablespoons canola oil, for brushing

1 tablespoon confectioners' sugar, for dusting

1. Preheat the oven to 375°F. Lightly grease four 4-inch tart pans.

2. Put the pumpkin or squash on a baking sheet and dot with the butter. Roast in the preheated oven for 5 minutes, then stir and return to the oven for an additional 20 minutes, or until the pumpkin is beginning to brown.

3. Stir the maple syrup, ginger, cinnamon, and allspice into the pumpkin and cook for an additional 5 minutes. Let cool.

4. Cut the pastry into twelve 4-inch squares. Brush four of the squares with oil. Place a second sheet of pastry on top of each, at an angle to the first so that the points of the squares do not align— you are aiming to create a star shape. Brush with oil again and repeat with the remaining pastry sheets to make four stacks, each with three layers.

5. Transfer the pastry stacks into the prepared pans, press down gently, and bake in the preheated oven for 8–10 minutes, or until crisp and golden.

6. Fill the pastry shells with the pumpkin mixture. Dust the tarts with the confectioners' sugar and serve immediately.

CHILE & AMARANTH
CORNBREAD

| **MAKES:** 1 loaf | **PREP TIME:** 20 mins | **COOK TIME:** 55 mins, plus cooling |

THE COMBINATION OF CORN AND CHILE BRINGS A NEW DYNAMIC TO CORNBREAD. IT CAN BE SERVED IN MANY WAYS, SUCH AS WITH SOUP, STEW, OR CHILI, WITH DEEP-FRIED CHICKEN, OR SIMPLY PAIRED WITH A FRESH SALAD.

INGREDIENTS

2–3 fresh red chiles, or to taste

¾ cup amaranth flour

¾ cup all-purpose white flour

¾ cup cornmeal

1 tablespoon baking powder

1 teaspoon baking soda

1½ teaspoons salt

¼ cup granulated sugar

1 cup shredded cheddar cheese

3 eggs

1 cup buttermilk

5 tablespoons butter, melted and cooled slightly, plus extra for greasing

⅓ cup fresh or frozen corn kernels, thawed if frozen

1. Preheat the oven to 400°F. Preheat the broiler and grease a 9 x 5-inch loaf pan.

2. Put the chiles under the preheated broiler and cook, turning occasionally, for 5–7 minutes, until blackened all over. Remove the skins and seeds and finely chop the flesh.

3. Sift together the amaranth flour, white flour, cornmeal, baking powder, baking soda, and salt into a large bowl. Stir in the sugar and cheese.

4. Whisk the eggs with the buttermilk and melted butter until well blended.

5. Make a well in the center of the flour mixture and pour in the egg mixture. Mix together with a fork, gradually drawing in the dry ingredients from the side.

6. Stir in the chiles and corn and spoon the batter into the prepared pan, leveling the surface. Bake in the preheated oven for 40–45 minutes, until a toothpick inserted into the center comes out clean.

7. Let cool in the pan for 10 minutes, then turn out onto a wire rack and let cool completely.

LIME & CHILE
SORBET ICE POPS

| MAKES: 8 | PREP TIME: 15 mins, plus cooling and freezing | COOK TIME: 10 mins |

THESE PALE, CHILE-SPECKLED SORBET STICKS ARE A TWIST ON THE CLASSIC LEMON SORBET—THEY HAVE A HIDDEN KICK FROM THE CHILE. FOR A LESS SPICY VERSION, REDUCE THE AMOUNT OF CHILE.

INGREDIENTS

½ cup superfine sugar
1 red chile, seeded and minced
1¾ cups water
4 large limes
8 thin slices from a small lime

1. Put the sugar, chile, and water into a saucepan. Put over medium–low heat, stirring, for 6–8 minutes, or until the sugar has dissolved. Increase the heat to medium–high and bring the mixture to a boil, then remove from the heat.

2. Finely grate the zest of two of the limes into the mixture and stir. Cover and let cool completely; this will take about 1 hour.

3. Squeeze the juice from the four limes and stir it into the mixture.

4. Pour the mixture into eight ¼-cup ice pop molds and place a lime slice into each mold. Insert the ice pop sticks and freeze for 5–6 hours, or until firm.

5. To unmold the ice pops, dip the frozen molds into warm water for a few seconds, and gently release the pops while holding the sticks.

CHILE & WASABI
BLOODY MARY

SERVES: 1	PREP TIME: 20 mins	COOK TIME: none

THIS ZINGY COCKTAIL OFFERS NO HALF MEASURES IN TERMS OF ITS HEAT. SAVORY COCKTAILS ARE THE NEW TREND, AND THIS VERSION OF BLOODY MARY, WITH CHILI POWDER, LIME JUICE, WASABI, AND BULLDOG SAUCE, WILL HIT THE SPOT.

INGREDIENTS

¾ ounce vodka

¾ ounce sake

½ ounce lime juice

½ teaspoon Korean chili powder

¼ teaspoon garlic granules

1-inch piece fresh ginger, grated

1 teaspoon Thai fish sauce

½ teaspoon wasabi paste

2 teaspoons tonkatsu bulldog sauce or other hot sauce

whole ice cubes

¾ cup tomato juice

daikon radish stick, to decorate

1. Mix together the vodka, sake, lime juice, chili powder, garlic granules, ginger, fish sauce, wasabi paste, and bulldog sauce in a Collins or highball glass, using a bar spoon.

2. Stir well, making sure all the ingredients are well combined.

3. Add a few ice cubes and the tomato juice and stir again.

4. Decorate with the daikon radish and serve immediately.

TIP
THIS IS A DELIGHT WHEN SERVED WITH OYSTERS—AND YOU CAN ADJUST THE SEASONINGS TO TASTE.

VEGETABLE TUMMY TREAT

SERVES: 1	PREP TIME: 15 mins	COOK TIME: none

WAKE UP YOUR BODY AND STIMULATE YOUR DIGESTIVE SYSTEM WITH THIS FRESH-TASTING ORANGE-AND-TOMATO DRINK. THERE IS ALSO A KICK IN THE TAIL DELIVERED BY THE CHILE TO SHAKE UP THOSE TASTE BUDS.

INGREDIENTS

3 oranges, zest and a little pith removed

1 carrot, halved

2 tomatoes, coarsely chopped

½ cup chilled water

1 small green chile, halved

2 celery stalks, thickly sliced

2 teaspoons hemp seed oil

1. Cut two oranges in half and feed them and the carrot through a juicer. Pour the juice into a blender. Coarsely chop and seed the remaining orange, then put it, the tomatoes, and water into the blender and process until smooth. Add the chile and celery and process again until blended. Pour into a glass, stir in the hemp seed oil, and serve.

INDEX